Mapping Social Relations

A Primer in Doing Institutional Ethnography

Mapping Social Relations
A Primer in Doing Institutional Ethnography

Marie Campbell
and
Frances Gregor

AltaMira Press

A Division of Rowman and Littlefield Publishers, Inc.
Walnut Creek Lanham New York Toronto Oxford

AltaMira Press
A Division of Rowman & Littlefield Publishers, Inc.
1630 North Main Street, #367
Walnut Creek, CA 94596
www.altamirapress.com

Rowman & Littlefield Publishers, Inc.
A Member of the Rowman & Littlefield Publishing Group
4501 Forbes Blvd, Suite 200
Lanham, MD 20706

ISBN 0-75910-752-1 (pbk.)
ISBN 0-75910-751-3 (bound)

Library of Congress Cataloging-in-Publication Data Available

Originally Published in Canada
by Garamond Press Ltd.
63 Mahogany Court,
Aurora. ON
L4G 6M8
www.garamond.ca

Canadian ISBN 1-55193-034-x

Printed in Canada

The paper used in this publication meets the minimum requirements of American National Standard for Information Sciences—Permanence of Paper for Printed Library Materials, ANSI/NISO Z39.48–1992.

Table of Contents

Introduction

Why Another "Methods" Text?

We decided to call this book on institutional ethnography a primer. Its purpose is to equip readers with the basic ideas and instructions to conduct research using this approach. Not only are we beginning at a basic level, we also want to make some rather complex ideas more accessible. There already exists a body of good theoretical writing about this approach to studying everyday life but our own students – mainly graduate students from the human service professions – wanted a different kind of resource for learning how to do institutional ethnography. They wanted a text to use in the classroom, and a guide to take away with them, as they went about researching topics of their own.

There are many kinds of methods texts on bookstands and in libraries. In the course of thinking about and writing this book, we have read a number of them. We have become interested in comparing different writers' attempts to explain research methods to students. Some texts, like this one, claim to make the topic easily understandable. And some of these efforts do make good reading. But sometimes the effort to make an accessible description of research methods or methodology ends up creating other problems. Writing about research methods offers a certain challenge because, to describe and compare methods from different theoretical traditions, the writer must be thoroughly familiar with them all. Students would certainly appreciate having one text that would tell them everything they needed to know about research methods but we are beginning to realize that, almost without exception, this is a false promise. We believe that it is more practicable, and certainly more modest, to try to write about methodology from one's own perspective. Many of the general methods texts we have read try to do too much – with confusing results. Sometimes, as in a new text that has come to hand, the writing is clear, the chapters, themes, and sections are logical, the illustrations are clever, and the exercises are interesting and helpful. But there is a drawback. Such a text can leave the reader with a false understanding of the subject. If readers really are committed to learning a practice of research that will hold up to scholarly scrutiny, books that attempt to explain all the qualitative methods, or all the ethnographies, in a few pages are likely to mislead. At least, that is our opinion.

Research builds on foundations of scholarship that themselves are always complex and ever-changing, and that are contested across disciplines, traditions, and schools of thought. It will be that way as long as there is no full agreement on the nature of the world in which we live and how to make sense of it. It seems only reasonable that a researcher who is good at what she does will write about research from her own perspective on knowledge. Besides writing in understandable language and all the other things that make for a good book, we are suggesting that it may be impossible to construct an account of research methods that is adequately and objectively comparative. The grounding assumptions of each method may be quite different, disorganizing the basis of comparison. That is why we feel that it makes sense to believe that the closer a writer sticks to her own specialty, the better her book will be. Which brings us back to this primer in mapping social relations.

This is a book about one methodological approach. It unapologetically argues the reasons why one would want to do this kind of research. Occasionally, for the sake of clarity, comparisons are drawn with how other methodologists speak about their research, their ideas, and their practices. But our purpose is not objective comparison among methods. Rather, this is one strategy we use to try to explain what our approach is all about. We are showing how to think about institutional ethnography in contrast to what other experts say about their approaches. Readers who have already been introduced to Dorothy Smith's writings will know that this little text does not contain the fullness of her thinking. It skims, selects, and interprets what Smith's own books develop more elegantly.[1] We expect that newcomers to the approach will discover that, after reading this text, they will want to read Smith's writings and as much of her students' work as they can find. Much of this work is referenced in the text.

2

About the Authors

Marie L. Campbell is the senior author. She is a professor at the University of Victoria and teaches in the interdisciplinary graduate program in the Faculty of Human and Social Development, "Studies in Policy and Practice in Health and Social Services." Campbell's background is in nursing and she studied sociology with Dorothy Smith at both the University of British Columbia and the Ontario Institute for Studies in Education in Toronto, Canada. Her research has employed institutional ethnography to study human service work organization. Beginning with her doctoral research – a study of management information systems being used in hospital nursing, successive institutional ethnographies have included analyses of an Ontario child protection agency, an Ontario college-based nursing education program, and a BC extended care hospital. Between 1996 and 1999 she led a collaborative inquiry into the health care experiences of people with disabilities in Victoria. Her teaching has been primarily in human service professional graduate schools – first Carleton University's School of Social Work, then in a multidisciplinary Master's program that admitted nurses, social workers, and child and youth care workers at the University of Victoria. Campbell has taught courses that introduce graduate students to the social organization of professional knowledge and to the critical analysis of professional practice that this approach makes possible. She has also supervised the thesis research of many students who are using institutional ethnography. It is mainly this teaching and supervision, and the students' research efforts, on which this text relies – for examples, exercises, and commentary.

Frances Gregor is the second author. She is an associate professor in the School of Nursing at Dalhousie University in Halifax, Canada. Although she teaches both graduate and undergraduate nursing students, her situation is rather different from that of her co-author. Gregor is beginning to integrate the social organization of knowledge and institutional ethnography in her teaching. Gregor began doctoral study in 1986, twenty years after qualifying as a registered nurse and fifteen years after beginning work as a university teacher of nurses. During these years her research interests were located squarely within a professional nursing discourse and she used traditional approaches to examine an activity that nurses call "patient education" (Gregor 1981, 1984). At the same time she was raising three children and was actively involved in policy-setting committees of a national voluntary health organization. In the early 1980s a growing feminist consciousness and awareness of the invisibility of her own work as mother, nurse, and volunteer, and of women's work generally, prompted her to return to study. Her discovery of Dorothy Smith's work and of institutional ethnography opened up the possibility of understanding how such invisibility was produced. In her doctoral research she returned once again to study nurses' work but from the perspective embodied in institutional ethnography (Gregor 1994). She is currently in the early stages of an analysis of the social relations of contemporary baccalaureate nursing education. Her own research commitments underpin her interest in learning how to communicate the relevance of institutional ethnography for professional human service workers. Not being a student of Smith's and not being trained as a sociologist, Gregor recognizes the struggle involved in understanding both the theory and method of institutional ethnography. That has not undermined her conviction that institutional ethnography is useful for nursing students. Her conviction enlivens her search for methods suitable to conveying this approach to her own students and to readers of this book. One of her contributions to the text has been her critical appraisal, in light of her developing use of the method, of its suggested instructions for beginning researchers.

By introducing ourselves here, we intend to help readers recognize how our various contributions to the text have emerged. You will find us speaking about ourselves in different ways. It is sometimes awkward to attribute pieces of writing to one or the other of us in the text and sometimes it is not important to do so. Where it does seem necessary, choosing the appropriate form of attribution has often been difficult. Sometimes, as now, it seems to feel right to speak as "we." At other times throughout the text, especially when referencing research or writing by one or other we revert to more formal characterization as "Campbell (1999) says ..." It may then seem appropriate to continue in that formal vein throughout that particular discussion of research. Sometimes, to attribute stories that we have each contributed, we appear as "Fran" or "Marie." Our biographies suggest what we each know and how this book takes its particular form.

Positioning the Text in Relation to its Users and Uses

This book takes its shape from the authors' experiences of teaching a particular population of university students. Students whose undergraduate education has prepared them to work as professionals in the human service disciplines look to graduate education for specific kinds of teaching and learning. They typically return to school in mid-career and, of course, they bring the personalities, the accumulated knowledge, and the motivations arising out of their practice of working with people. Their location is in a society with a shifting public commitment to the welfare state. They are members of a profession in which they are practised in relating to people who are their clients. In their jobs, they would have been involved in the scope of human experience that professionals are positioned to encounter – we can imagine them helping to manage illness and death, and intervening in situations of interpersonal violence, poverty, and deprivation. As front-line workers, they share in their clients' moments of joy, anger, hope, fear, pain, and despair. They might have been engaged in conceptualizing, planning, and organizing efforts to improve difficult life situations. It is likely that, for many students, the professionalized character of their work would have shaped them, their own ways of knowing, and what they deem important. Some would have been immersed in highly bureaucratic work settings, where their success depends upon identifying and learning to adapt to specific organizational culture and routines. Added to the ordinary stresses of their work settings and the effects of the troubles that they encounter, they are likely to see and be concerned about doing important work that is socially undervalued and too often under-resourced.

All these elements coalesce to shape the people who return to school and they determine what kind of learner the students will be. They may be very highly motivated, intent on learning how to improve their practice and make changes to society. As graduate students, they tend not to be naïve and not particularly deferent or compliant. They are likely to be focused and practical about course choices. They are often balancing part-time work and family responsibilities with their studies. Women predominate in these fields, many are single parents, and universities offer little in the way of financial support for graduate education in the human services. Students' efficient use of time is therefore crucial.

Graduate curricula in the human services must reflect and respond to all these exigencies. To work well for the students, what is taught and how it is taught must be clearly relevant to their lives and interests. Programs must be flexible as an acknowledgement of the actualities within which these students operate. The curriculum of the graduate program that Campbell has been instrumental in designing explicitly makes the students' own knowledge and experiences central to the courses. Critical and analytic traditions and skills are introduced within the context of what students already know and how they can make use of new knowledge. The pedagogical goal is to bring theory into the classroom in such a way as to illuminate what students are concerned about. This is in contrast to teaching an academic subject where the discourse determines its themes and their boundaries, and identifies its important contributors. In Campbell's program, research is taught as a tool for extending the student/practitioner's reach – both expanding their understanding and increasing their capacity to act on issues of practical relevance.

Institutional ethnography appears remarkably well suited to such a human service graduate curriculum. Its strategy for learning how to understand problems existing in everyday life appeals to many human service workers. For students who want to make changes in actual situations that they know are not working well for people, institutional ethnography may be a useful choice. Yet, at the same time, its highly elaborated theoretical foundation is difficult to deal with in the brief time these students are in the Master's level classroom. For us, it has seemed useful to try to work out the content of a body of knowledge that is just sufficient for students to undertake studies in this approach. We ask ourselves how we can teach institutional ethnography in as efficient a manner as possible. We have both been testing out instructional methods and materials. This book is the product of our efforts.

Although our experience as instructors has been mainly with students in the human services, we hope that the text will appeal to more than just instructors and students in these fields. We recognize the special characteristics and learning needs of our own students and it is easy to see how institutional ethnography is appropriate. For students of the human services, the compatibility is between their professional goals and the activist-orientation of the process and product of analysis. Human service workers are likely to benefit from learning more specifically how the programmed activities in their fields are put together with whatever outcomes. They may benefit from learning how participants in the research settings bring into being (and make "real") something that otherwise seems to exist in words, ideas, directives, and policy – that is, in virtual form. If a student is researching a setting that she knows well, such insights about its practical features may also generate confidence and hope for making things work better, where little hope existed before. Or the analysis may entirely re-orientate a student/practitioner's thinking about a problem and suggest alternative ways to work for change. We are of the opinion that this kind of goal for research is likely to resonate with many students in the social sciences and also with community activists. We expect that our examples drawn from the human services can easily be converted, in reading, into situations familiar to the interested reader.

How the Book Is Organized

Chapter One situates the budding institutional ethnographer in the stance that she will take to the topic to be studied. The message in this chapter is that learning institutional ethnography commits researchers to a particular way of looking. There is something distinctive not only about *how* the institutional ethnographer looks at the world but what she *looks for*. Knowing involves a relation between the researcher and what is known. She asks and sets out to discover: "How does this happen as it does? How are these relations organized?" Institutional ethnographers cannot step out of their bodies and histories to know "in general." They explore the everyday world. Chapter One suggests how a novice institutional ethnographer might get "a feel" for the approach. Campbell and Gregor draw from their teaching experience to offer illustrations about where to begin.

Institutional ethnography is a methodology that turns Dorothy Smith's social organization of knowledge into a research practice. Chapter Two introduces, explains, and illustrates some theoretical terms that are important to that theorized way of knowing the everyday world. Thus, we begin with social relations and social organization, and progress on to text-mediated social organization, discursively-organized and objectified knowing, and their use in ruling practices. We draw our examples from stories we have used in classes, and excerpts of the writings of other institutional ethnographers.

Chapter Three begins a detailed discussion of the research process of institutional ethnography. We are assuming that readers are consulting this book as they prepare to undertake a study using this method. Our discussion of how to do institutional ethnography begins at a project's proposal stage. Here we introduce the term *problematic* and its use in institutional ethnography. We draw on Dorothy Smith's (1987) instructions about focusing research attention on puzzles emerging in everyday life, as actual people experience them. An inquiry grows from what a researcher makes problematic and the topic of further exploration. After that, and still thinking of the proposal, we address the question of doing a literature review. Reviewing the literature is a standard requirement for research writing, so much so that while it might seem tedious, it is otherwise not considered troublesome. Nothing could be further from the truth in institutional ethnography. Its theoretical grounding in the social organization of knowledge complicates institutional ethnography's relation to all scholarship. Chapter Three explains how an institutional ethnographer reads the literature, not necessarily for information, but to analyze how the work of intellectuals has helped to give shape to the topic of interest. Institutional ethnographers do not cede authority to the literature, as scholars conventionally do. Finally, the chapter includes a discussion of how one's methodology is described, first in a proposal, and then again in the research report or thesis.

Chapter Four is about data, access to data, and data collection. Issues of access bring with them routine procedures for ensuring ethical treatment of research subjects. The chapter contains a discussion of how standard practices for demonstrating that their research is ethical may create special problems for institutional ethnographers. Going on to data collection, we note that the various kinds of ethnographic research use similar data collection techniques. We review how interviewing, observations, and documents are used in institutional ethnography. Because the analytic approach is to explicate what actually happens, good, careful, and detailed accounts of everyday life are needed to discover ways of entering into the analysis as an institutional ethnographer does. We write about needing to access two levels of data. Beyond the ethnographic accounts that describe experiences, the researcher must also work back to see how those experiences happened as they did. Thus, second-level data is collected in order to make the social relations of settings explicable.

Chapter Five explains and discusses theoretical and practical issues of analysis in institutional ethnography. There is more to this analysis than producing a thorough, accurate and lively picture of a setting and of the topic under study. Institutional ethnography does not develop a theory from the data nor does it collapse ethnographic description into generic concepts, categories or themes. This chapter uses a comparative strategy to make explication – the goal of analysis in institutional ethnography – understandable, and gives examples that suggest the usefulness of explicating experiential data. The chapter explains the importance of beginning an inquiry into something arising in a subject's experience and mapping the socially-organized conditions of that experience. In addition, some strategies for facing the task of writing analysis are offered. The challenge is not just to make sense of data following the dictates of this approach, but to make the analysis persuasive. It must account for what actually happened or happens. The analytic story told must supply convincing evidence of what is being argued.

In Chapter Six we summarize some exemplary writings in this field to show what can be done using the method. The book's premise is that institutional ethnography is an approach to knowing about the social world that is useful for people who have an interest in furthering democracy where they live, upholding values that they think are worth struggling for. We are often confused about how best to do that. We read, watch TV, worry, and discuss our lives and public and private events with our friends and colleagues. Some of us do research. Institutional ethnography is an analytic approach that begins where we are – as actual people with bodies located in time and space. It offers a theorized approach to reflecting critically on what one knows from that embodied place in the world. In this chapter we show some of the efforts that institutional ethnographers are making to critically and analytically examine puzzles emerging from their own and other people's lives. We may want to work on private problems that pain others or ourselves, or perhaps we are moving towards addressing inequities experienced by larger groups. In either case, institutional ethnography can contribute to understanding how to respond to oppressions of all kinds. The examples that we offer in Chapter Six address diverse topics: experiences of international development, palliative care, disabilities policy in a university, an immigrant women's job placement centre, conducting institutional ethnography as a participatory or collaborative endeavour, analyzing the course of a social movement. We hope that these accounts inspire your efforts to study your own puzzles and learn how to make our world a better place to live in.

Acknowledgements

The first and most important acknowledgement is to Dorothy E. Smith, whose years of commitment to the women's movement and to scholarship have resulted in her development of the research methods that we use, adapt for our own purposes, and talk about here. Her work is the basis for a sociology that makes it possible for people to understand the apparently inexplicable organization of their own and other people's everyday lives. Smith was Professor at the Ontario Institute for Studies in Education at the University of Toronto when her first four books were published. A fifth book, on analyzing textual practices, is currently in progress. Smith's work has always been directed to audiences and purposes outside of academe. She has spoken of her work as mapping social relations. "Although some of the work of inquiry must be technical, as making a map is, its product would be ordinarily accessible and usable, just as a map is"(Smith 1999, 95). That has become our goal for this text. We intend our account of mapping social relations to be ordinarily accessible and usable.

We are especially indebted to our students and colleagues who have taught us much that we have come to know – not only about teaching but also about writing and using institutional ethnography. Teaching and supervising students who are keen to learn is a privilege that we both enjoy. It forces us to rethink words that roll off the tongue but that may not really make sense to a class or a reader. Making meaning, as Smith says, is dialogic and for the wonderful dialogues we have both been part of, many thanks to our students and colleagues.

Chapter One

Finding a Place to Begin

Practices of Knowing, Forms of Literacy

Newcomers to institutional ethnography must learn how to look at their research topics rather differently than if they were doing conventional research. For anyone who has received scholarly training, this means identifying and unlearning some common assumptions about research and accepted practices of knowing. The student of institutional ethnography is required, for instance, to see herself as a knower located in the everyday world and finding meaning there, in contrast to reliance on library research[2] and the application of theories – what we would see as remaining "in the discourse." As instructors of institutional ethnography ourselves, this is where our teaching begins. We plan classes that open up for discussion our students' practices of thinking, reading, and reflecting on their own experiences and knowledge. Through that, we teach an orientation to research as an opportunity for students to inquire into topics that are meaningful to them and to make inquiry a process of discovery. Institutional ethnography is a theorized way of seeing and knowing that re-orientates people in their everyday world. Employing this theorized process of discovery helps institutional ethnographers see "how it works," so important elements can be mapped. To begin a discussion of how seeing and knowing are theorized in institutional ethnography we first borrow some ideas from Richard Darville[3] (1995) who has said much the same things to a different audience. Then we describe some teaching methods that we use.

The framework that Darville proposes to literacy teachers for their teaching is useful for our purposes in a number of ways. For one thing, it shows how knowledge and power come together in the everyday world to organize what happens to people. That is important to us, too, because, as in literacy work, institutional ethnography attempts to make the world more understandable to ordinary people. Literacy work has a long history of commitment to the empowerment of the oppressed and disadvantaged (for example, Freire 1972). Like literacy teaching, institutional ethnography draws on local experiences in confronting and analyzing how people's lives come to be dominated and shaped by forces outside of them and their purposes. Darville introduces to literacy teaching a process of reading that goes beyond the technical skills of reading and writing and adds a theorized approach to confronting knowledge practices. He argues that it matters to those who try to read it that knowledge is put together for different purposes.

Darville notes the importance of experience – his own teaching experience and the experiences of literacy students that literacy teachers use in their instruction. Following Dorothy Smith (1984), Darville points out that knowing is anchored in particular places and particular uses. By recognizing that grounding, readers can make sense of the particular form of literacy being employed. He analyzes the practices of thinking and knowing that literacy students are routinely taught and he dissects how they fail in some situations. He argues that anybody can be rendered illiterate and powerless when they face writing that is constructed for purposes that are mysterious to the reader. Organizational memos may read like a foreign language to employees when not related to their own work. Or applicants for a first job may misunderstand what is wanted and write "the wrong thing" in the application form.

Darville identifies the literacy methods and skills that turn literacy students into political actors and he claims that anything less is really not a satisfactory goal for literacy teaching. Institutional ethnographers make the same claim for doing research. Again, Darville's process for teaching literacy is instructive for institutional ethnographers. Literacy teachers routinely ask students to tell and then learn to write down stories from their own lives. His critique of this literacy teaching method is that its focus is on a form of literacy he calls "narrative." Students learn to find meaning in the sequence of events told or written as the knower experienced them. Darville thinks that literacy instruction should guide adult literacy students towards making sense of everyday lives that are embedded (as is everybody's life) in what he calls organizational literacy. He argues that the way that big organizations employ written materials of all kinds to get their work done is a particular form of literacy. Although working with their own experience is certainly important, students being taught to read and write also need to be shown the significance of *"how things get written up"* (for organizational action) (Darville 1995, 254, his emphasis). Formatted entirely differently from narrative accounts, organizational literacy collects, categorizes, and uses knowledge for organizational purposes. When literacy students see this distinction, they can begin to understand why organizational texts and textual processes are incomprehensible to them. Gaining the skills to see how power works through special institutional forms of knowing, they can begin to take more control of their lives. Institutional ethnography, like literacy teaching, makes use of Darville's notion that people can learn skills to engage successfully with dominant forms of literacy, and even draw on their own experiential knowledge to resist domination. When they do they too can insist that organizations serve them rather than just manage them.

In this chapter, and as you engage with institutional ethnography, we suggest that you try to put aside how you have been previously trained to do scholarly work, and open yourself to a new practice. There are new skills of discovery and mapping to be learned. Yet, newcomers to institutional ethnography share with literacy learners an important indigenous knowledge resource – the language of experience. In Darville's long-range view for literacy teaching, the tools of seeing how things work can be combined to good effect with literacy learners' own experiential knowledge of their own lives. Having experienced life as an adult unable to read, they already know a good deal about being subordinated. This knowledge is anchored where they live and have suffered. With that specific experience as a ground, and employing their new practices for engaging with organizational literacy, they can speak up about what works for them and what does not.

The Located Knower: A Feminist Discovery

When students arrive in research classes they bring themselves and their histories into the learning setting. As Darville argues, all knowing is grounded somewhere. This applies to students, too, a point that must be made a central topic for discussion about institutional ethnography. Otherwise it fades, or rather it never emerges from the depths of a student's consciousness. The conventions of research methodology that permeate all scholarship, indeed all education, have for centuries treated the researcher's presence as a problem that must be overcome. Dorothy Smith's work in the social organization of knowledge is the product of her struggle against the hegemony of this scholarship. Beyond debates about positivism, Smith's research was affected by her developing feminist consciousness and her involvement in the women's movement of the 1970s (see, for example, Smith 1977). Smith was one of the feminist scholars of that time who had come to see that women were not adequately represented by the forms of knowledge that claimed to be speaking about them. Feminists recognized that the research being conducted within their disciplines failed themselves and other women – Smith and others proposed new ways of looking at the accepted and authoritative methods of knowing. Smith's *Everyday World as Problematic: A Feminist Sociology* (1987) put institutional ethnography into the scholarly discourse. By then, feminist methodology had become the centre of a lively and extended debate that has gone on to revolutionize intellectual work.

In the 1970s and 1980s, many women who had experienced the feminist movement went to university in the hope of breaking out of the ways of knowing that confined them to, and then rationalized, their oppressive positions. In Canada and elsewhere, feminist students from many disciplines were attracted to the ideas in Smith's writings and to the research approach she taught. Other students besides those working on women's issues saw the usefulness of institutional ethnography in addressing oppressions of various kinds (see Campbell and Manicom 1995; Diamond 1992; Swift 1995). Smith's subsequent writing, and that of other institutional ethnographers, has continued to attract politically-engaged students. The potential for the marriage of scholarly research and political engagement remains a motivation for successive generations of students working in institutional ethnography. This primer may be useful to those who already know about institutional ethnography and are looking for some practical instruction on conducting a study. But our motivation for writing has been primarily to engage with newcomers to institutional ethnography. If you are new to institutional ethnography, we are hoping to talk to you.

Graduate students arriving in research classes by a different route from most feminist or activist students have particular learning needs. You begin your research training from your own place with particular background experiences and expectations. For instance, many of you in the human service disciplines come to graduate school for a career-enhancing credential. Of course, some of you are also feminists or activists within your own occupations and communities but you are unlikely to have sought out your educational program on the basis of the approach to research it offers. You may approach research as a requirement for the completion of a degree rather than being related to working with your own practical problems. In such situations, it is up to us as instructors to make the possibilities of institutional ethnography understandable and attractive. This creates a particular set of teaching challenges.

Instructors must learn how to make explicit the idea, central to institutional ethnography, that doing research of any kind commits you to a certain social relation. This view of knowing, that it relates us to others in a specific way, is part of institutional ethnography's theory of knowledge. As students you must see that by virtue of what you know and how you take up your exploration that you are located *vis à vis* other people. Rather than treating a knower's location as a problem of bias, we believe that it reveals something about whose interests are served. And that is an issue of power. To explore how knowing relates to power, institutional ethnographers study how one's knowing is organized – by whom and by what. To elaborate on this, let's go back to Darville.

In the literacy field, empowerment of students is an accepted part of the instructional goal. Darville claimed that literacy students' location as outsiders to organizational literacy is a problem that their teachers have to recognize and address. The literacy teacher, as part of her training and practice, takes for granted that her students are disadvantaged by their lack of literacy skills. Darville argued that the conventional methods of literacy teaching (working on their own narrative accounts) would fail students unless teachers recognized an additional responsibility – that is, showing students how organizational literacy *dominates* them. Darville shows that to empower students fully, literacy needs to be taught as a form of social analysis. Students can learn to see how power is carried in knowledge. In this recommendation, Darville was introducing a theorized way of reading particular language and texts arising in big organizations where their use is a form of power. Darville's framework for analysis allows literacy teachers and students to see that the externally-organized world would always remain puzzling and dominating if students relied on canvassing their own experiences and that of their friends. More than a story about something, an organizational text is organizing a relation. The reader/knower is captured through participation. Resistance to being dominated in that relation must begin by the reader recognizing how institutional domination and subordination work. Not understanding an organization is one form of domination. Understanding it and having it shape a course of action is another.

Teaching institutional ethnography includes discovering and analyzing institutional relations of power. As research instructors faced with introducing institutional ethnography to our classes, we have more to think about than the ordinary job of teaching, inspiring, and encouraging. We also have the task of showing students how to recognize and analyze the relations of power within which you live and work. Your capacity to do institutional ethnography depends upon this, and this will become apparent as you read this book. While you may not immediately recognize research as a political undertaking, the politics of knowing are not likely to be foreign to you in your practice of the human services.

Those of you who are nurses, for instance, work in environments that are politically highly charged. While the effects of institutional power pervade nurses' work lives, the negative effects may appear to individual nurses simply as personal problems. As a nurse, you may feel that your working relations are troubled owing to the personalities, competence or incompetence of your co-workers or superiors. For some nurses a sense of injustice pervades your work life. You may feel that although you do vital work, it remains unrecognized and unappreciated. Nurses sometimes speak of themselves and their work as being invisible to others in the field of health care and also to the public. It may be that at this pre-political point you decide to become a graduate student. As your instructors, we need to show you that research knowledge may be a tool for social justice. Or, conversely, it may be a tool for managing and ordering people in conformity with interests, neither yours nor theirs. The difference is built in to the standpoint taken. As you go further into this book you will learn that institutional ethnography "takes the standpoint of those who are being ruled."

If you are a graduate student of research methods and a human service worker, you may be beginning your studies in a different place from the graduate student who is an activist. However, the same features of institutional ethnography are likely to interest you both. Institutional ethnography offers the capacity to look at the everyday world and figure out and "map" how things happen the way they do. We explore how relations between people establish the world, and how we know it and live in it. When we claim in this book to be offering a primer in mapping social relations, we are naming that task of exploration and discovery in the everyday world. Instructors of newcomers to institutional ethnography have to find the words, exercises, and examples that allow you to see your research interests in relation to the realities of people's lives.

Challenging Authoritative Ways of Knowing

The established scholarly way of validating knowledge is to reference authorities. Students learn to couch their ideas in a stream of scholarship that continually reconstitutes themes, concepts, and theories. New findings must be built up from and refer back to ideas already established in the literature. Institutional ethnography, drawing on a feminist critique of scholarship, challenges this approach to knowing and offers an alternative (Smith 1987). One way of describing research in institutional ethnography is to say that to understand our lives, or the lives of other people, we must find the actual determinations of those life conditions and "map them." As students, you have to have a feel for what that means and how to do it. As instructors introducing the approach, we must communicate what is vital about the mapping project. Locating *the actual* as a distinct terrain of inquiry is one of the first challenges. We can hint at it by saying that underlying anyone's everyday life experience, something invisible is happening to generate a particular set of circumstances. It is that "something" that is of research interest. People's lives happen in real time and in real locations to real people. Institutional ethnographers explore the actual world in which things happen, in which people live, work, love, laugh, and cry. Exploring that is a different research undertaking from approaches that objectify people and events, and slot them into theoretical categories to arrive at explanation. As already suggested, our theory commits us not to theoretical explanations, but to certain theorized practices of looking at the actualities of everyday life. Institutional ethnographers believe that people and events are *actually* tied together in ways that make sense of such abstractions as power, knowledge, capitalism, patriarchy, race, the economy, the state, policy, culture, and so on. But for newcomers to institutional analysis, this primary attempt to describe and explain institutional ethnography may be still too abstract to be very meaningful.

We have experimented with how to offer instruction that illustrates institutional ethnography's principles. We want our students to appreciate how their own experiences matter to the research and how the research process is learned. We want to demonstrate how you will be learning to unravel your own and other people's experiences, to discover how they are put together. Clearly, this requires us to be interested in who our students are, what you know and what puzzles you. As graduate students coming back to university from jobs in the human services you come neither empty-handed nor empty-headed. And you do not bring only abstract understandings. Besides your integration of concepts, theories, and skills from your undergraduate education, your background of work

17

experience means that you have a store of "real-life" stories and questions. Students like you routinely have explanations, as well as queries about these explanations. Yet, often the understandings that your education has provided are not sufficiently coherent with your work experiences to be entirely satisfactory. Your professional theories may be out of step with the settings in which you work and with your clients and colleagues. You may not have the conceptual tools to bring the divergent pieces of your work together.

Learning to See "Social Organization" in a Health Care Setting

Fran Gregor works with graduate nursing students to help them to reflect on their practice of nursing in a process of storytelling, discussion, and exploration. Fran introduces her objective as creating an opportunity for nursing students to analyze their experiences as women and professional workers in contemporary health care settings. She assigns readings showing their profession, its knowledge and practices, and their work settings as "socially organized." (This is a concept that, up until now in this chapter, we have referred to in standard language; here we are using it to mean "things being put together systematically, but more or less mysteriously and outside a person's knowledge, and for purposes that may not be theirs.") In telling their stories, students draw from experiences that have created tension or anxiety for themselves and others. As with Darville's literacy learners, these nursing students tell stories about what happened to them or to those around them. But as Darville argued, experiential accounts, important as they are for locating the subject in relation to what happened, are inadequate as analysis. Fran moves her students towards analysis by inspiring them to ask questions and focus an inquiry on "what actually happened."

Assigned readings help to short cut the teaching of the theories of knowledge behind institutional ethnography. The readings (for example, institutional ethnographies of similar nursing topics or of analogous situations) offer students some insights into "how to look" at their own experiences as "socially organized." Once they grasp "how to look," their storytelling becomes more focused for a particular analysis, one that is theorized. The theory that is being employed, although implicitly, is Smith's social organization of knowledge (Smith 1990a; 1990b). Latour and Woolgar (1979) point out about science that accepted "ways of looking" are turned into instruments that have generations of theory embedded in them. When scientific instruments are

18

used, so is the theory, although it is taken for granted by users. We consider our approach to teaching institutional ethnography as reliant on theory in somewhat similar ways. Students learn from other institutional ethnographers how to "see" their settings sufficiently well to follow the institutional ethnographer's lead in an actual process of discovery. In Fran's class, students write a paper to show how they are learning to come to terms with their experiences in this new "social organization" way.

The following is a paraphrased version of the story told by one of Fran's students, whom we will call Jan. Jan is employed as a nurse assessor in the Extra Mural Hospital Program in New Brunswick.[4] She assesses patients, either in a hospital or at their home, to determine their proper placement in programs of non-acute care – either a Special Care Home or Nursing Home. The work of assessing the patients' needs for continuing care is contracted out to nurses like Jan by the provincial government. The assessment process involves both nurses and social workers. A forty-seven-page text titled *New Brunswick Assessment and Continuing Care Instrument* is the tool used to determine a level of care for each patient. It requires the assessor to use a combination of narrative statements and tickboxes in a range of categories describing the patient's physical and mental status, housing, and so on. A referral by a physician, a nurse from the Extra Mural Hospital, a family member or friend triggers the assessment. The assessment can proceed only if the patient gives consent, and because it involves a decision about a public subsidy, consent to disclosing financial information must also be given.

Jan's story about her work had focused on concerns arising in relation to gaining consent for the assessment. Arriving at someone's home to do an assessment, she would often find that the patient did not expect her and did not know why she was there. This would be awkward for her and upsetting for the prospective patient. She found that her job of assessing included the delicate counselling role of getting people to the point of accepting an assessment for placement in a continuing care program. She recognized that even proposing the assessment made clients anxious and, for example, made them worried that their autonomy was at stake. In introducing the assessment, Jan entered into the potentially troubled and troubling aspects of the patient's family relations. She felt the burden of this, saying about her approach to the job: "I have to go very slowly, very carefully, so as not to upset (the person). It may take several visits (to complete the assessment) as I try to get to know them."

As a resource for analyzing her experience, Jan read several papers that Fran made available, bringing institutional ethnography to bear on nurses' work and health care organization. She used analyses by Campbell (1994; 2000) and Campbell and Jackson (1992) who introduce the idea of nurses' work being conceptualized and written up in particular ways to make it, and health care, manageable. These readings make particular kind of critique. In the situations analyzed, Campbell and Jackson are showing nurses actively involved in translating their nursing knowledge into textual forms that have an administrative purpose. Sometimes the form to be filled is part of a technology to organize the efficient use of nurses' time. Other forms capture accounts of nurses' work in order to evaluate it. In any case, the conclusion drawn is that when nurses "write up" their practice into organizationally programmed accounts, they begin to think about their work in the terms they are given. Filling in forms is more than a technical task. It draws nurses into the dominant practices of hospital management as its agents.

Even though systematized information has become a mainstay of hospital management and hospital nursing, nurses still intervene in patient treatment on the basis of their own professional judgement and individual assessments of patients, according to Campbell (2000). She argues that nurses' own intelligent, on-the spot interventions, often rescue from failure the operation of text-based strategies that are put in place to improve hospital efficiency. (One of her examples is of a nurse reviewing and enhancing a family practitioner's management of out-patient chemotherapy treatments to ensure patient safety.) Implicitly, nurses are counted on to bring their knowledge to bear on problems that would otherwise cause trouble for doctors, patients, and the efficient running of the whole system. Far from being recognized as crucial for hospital efficiency, that sort of contribution is mainly overlooked and Campbell argues that doing so supports efforts to apply management efficiencies to *nursing work*. It is convenient to understand nurses' work as tasks that can be defined and assigned (to variously trained staff) and to ignore that registered nurses' discretionary action helps keep health care settings running smoothly and safely. With text-based strategies in place, hospitals begin to treat their information-based systems as if they work on their own. That gives hospital management the confidence to reduce their nursing staff.

Nurses commonly work in ways that are not officially noticed and may even be illegitimate, as when nurses' knowledge and action strays across professional boundaries. Campbell (2000) describes nurses employing discrete "intelligent action" in order to provide the most appropriate, and safest, treatment for a patient – the nurse will use her knowledge and experience to interpret the physician's instructions in a way that will best meet the needs of the patient. She proposes that nurses' capacity to work around such delicate issues of what they should and should not know and do is a practice of gender relations in which the nursing profession is steeped. Nurses apply these skills to shoring up standard treatment regimens and making them fit an individual patient's needs. They go round in circles fixing the flaws in abstracted (textual) organization of patient care and then cover their tracks in accordance with the traditional gender regime. When the work they do is not part of the official and textual organization of nursing, it tends to be overlooked, thus not attributable to them as their knowledge, judgement or action. As suggested above, this may create even more trouble for nurses. When it appears that "the system" runs efficiently on the basis of abstract information, they may find their jobs being cut.

Fran's goal of having her students see the "social organization" in their stories helped Jan learn how to look at her own experiences analytically. The assigned readings help newcomers to the methodology "get a feel for" the kind of inquiry they might undertake. While skimming over the complex and sophisticated theory of the methodology, the readings turn students' attention to the everyday world looking for "how things work." In her first assignment, Jan began to look into what her work was accomplishing in New Brunswick's long-term care system. She began to identify what it meant for a patient to be assessed. She had been aware that the assessment form made everyone "look alike," what she referred to as "standardizing" patients. She could see that at times the assessment form "did not serve the needs of the patient all that well." Patients sometimes landed between the categories of the form where, in her view, the official reading of their eligibility might be wrong – and even inadequate for that particular individual. She also became aware of her own mediating influence on the scores that determined eligibility levels and that she could "dress a Level 2 up as a Level 3" to offer what she thought an individual needed. She also saw that eligibility criteria were not pegged to constant levels of funding. Those in charge of the program could, and did, "raise the bar" at any point when program costs were to be reduced. This would trump her own capacity to express a client's needs in assessment levels.

Fran's introduction of social organization to her nursing students takes up Darville's recommendation (to literacy teachers) to help students learn to how to engage with organizational texts. Theoretical concepts of the social organization of knowledge in the assigned readings are placed within a context familiar to nursing students. But the readings do more for Fran's students than show situations that are analogous to their own. They are also introducing a theorized way of looking at experiences. Darville's work in literacy, examined earlier in the chapter, makes the connection between knowledge and power in which institutional ethnographers are interested. In what he called organizational literacy, he saw that an organization's texts are constructed in ways that control and disempower people. For Jan, besides recognizing the way that an assessment suppressed the subjectivity of the person being assessed, what Jan called "standardizing" them, she was also introduced to how assessments work as a cost-cutting technique. Recognizing this would help her begin to understand the theoretical terms "ruling" and "ruling practices" and recognize them as operating through her own assessment work. Reflecting on her own participation in textual practices, she would see how professionals like herself could become agents of New Brunswick's agenda of cost-cutting, involuntarily visiting additional costs on old or disabled people. She would be able to see herself participating in a social relation of dominance and subordination.

As Jan becomes a novice institutional ethnographer, she is learning how organizational power is exercised in special forms of knowledge. As with most practitioners, she needs help in recognizing how she becomes entangled in ruling relations in the course of her routine conduct of assessments. Dorothy Smith's (1990) writings on the social organization of knowledge show how ubiquitous are the texts of contemporary society that are employed to process people and manage aspects of their lives. Working in textual media has become taken for granted and a routine competence for most people. The step across the boundary into ruling practices is usually obscured and has to be made a topic of inquiry. Jan would then see how an inquiry using institutional ethnography locates her not just as an unwitting participant, but as a critic of an authorized view – in this case of assessment information and health care policy. She would also query authoritative accounts of nurses' work that overlook, as her own work of assessment does, nurses' important contributions. Understanding that her background knowledge, professional judgement, knowledge, and skills had been essential to making the assessment, she would recognize that this work is not only invisible as nursing work, *but as ruling practice*. As instructors, we try to make creative use of any such contradictions in students' experiences as opportunities for teaching institutional ethnography's theorized way of looking and knowing. For students like

Jan, coming to terms with the troubling aspects of their everyday lives means learning how they are implicated in bringing those situations into being.

Embodied Knowing in a Text-Mediated World

Students have to learn that inquiry in institutional ethnography is about them and their ways of knowing. Or rather, as institutional ethnographers, they cannot stand apart from what they know and what they learn about the world. This is because (according to the social organization of knowledge) they *enact* the world they inhabit and know about, in concert with other people and, of course, with the technologies that people operate. This important theoretical and practical point has somehow to be absorbed by newcomers to the method. Marie Campbell has experimented with how to create opportunities for students to discover this for themselves. Marie teaches a course that brings into students' critical awareness their own competence as knowers and actors in highly textualized environments. Students are required to pay attention to themselves as embodied knowers and to their practices of reading a variety of texts.[5]

The following is an illustration of how the course proceeds. Marie introduces her mainly white, middle-class students to reading and writing activities that make the conditions of their own knowing available for consideration. She asks what it means to our interpretations of events and interactions, and to our certainty about our views, that we are white, for instance? Or non-disabled? Or heterosexual? Or women? Or professionally trained? Early in the course, a reading on whiteness (Kivel 1996) is assigned. Students in human service professions are likely to have been taught to practice, among other professional approaches, "cultural sensitivity" and the tenets of non-discriminatory or anti-racist practice. But they may not recognize how their own backgrounds, whatever they are, have inculcated and continually organize the positions in the world from which they "see" and know. Students may learn anti-racist and anti-oppressive tenets and practice them faithfully but they may not have learned to recognize the historical conditioning and continuing institutional enforcement of their knowing that stems from living in their own bodies in specific places and under specific conditions in the world. That recognition becomes a course objective.

Using students' own experiences is the basis for the systematic and self-reflective practice of knowing that is taught in the course. In a text-mediated world, people not only interact face-to-face, they also interact through texts. Being "knowing subjects" is where knowing begins. As Dorothy Smith (1990a,

28) has insisted in writing about her feminist methodology, people know through having a body and a consciousness. Even reading is not just an intellectual exercise. As an entry to reflection on their reading practices, students are asked to analyze how assigned readings are themselves socially organized. The readings (texts) have an author whom the students can "meet," learning about him or her from the text. This author is also a knowing subject located somewhere in the world, and again, this is discoverable from clues in the text. As reading, writing, and discussion in class ensue, students are encouraged to hear the range of responses to issues that the readings introduce. They disagree, of course, on how to make sense of what they read.[6] They are invited to contemplate that whatever response they have is *their* response and it stands as a marker of where they are now and where they have been in the world. When someone is impatient with what they see as other students' intransigence about their privileged positions, for instance, these divergent responses reflect the social location of both. Students' journal writing on assigned readings offers the instructor an opportunity to comment on and bring into view how students' histories organize their own reading practices and what they come to know, believe, reject, and so on.

The course instruction works on several levels simultaneously. It introduces analytic concepts, such as "embodied knowing," as relevant to a process of knowing that is an alternative to accepting external authority, for instance. Even though a lesson on embodied knowing need not be about "race," as suggested above, some substantive topic is opened up in each assigned reading and its discussion. The course explores oppressions as happening in the routine exercise of power. It may be easier for students (or anyone) to hold the view that oppression and domination are the products of morally reprehensible people acting badly. (The class might agree that that also happens). Yet, in this course, and beginning with their own reading and writing, students consider actual settings that they inhabit and explore how things actually happen there. On this analytic basis students learn how their own knowing is socially organized.

Because Marie's students generally have a background in the human services, they introduce stories from their own knowledge of everyday life in bureaucratic settings. Understanding the textual architecture of routine organizational action is crucial to institutional ethnography. Assigned readings include Dorothy Smith's (1975; 1990) work on "textual reality" and its effects in many bureaucratic and professional situations of text-mediated action. These readings show how the particular use of words, language and texts build organizational versions of what people say, do or know for organizational action. Reading Smith introduces students to the argument that it is a mistake to treat texts as transparent (Smith 1975). Her work problematizes that kind of reading. She argues that textualizing events and people's words and actions changes them. It may, for instance, translate them into official and bureaucratic accounts that become the groundwork for various forms of managerial and professional action. Smith's writings display the everyday elements of power when power is carried in texts.

Students reading Smith's work recognize that in their own organizational roles, they too get their work done using specially formatted language and texts. They see that exercising control over the form that knowledge takes is central to their own experiences and their own success as well as the troubles they identify in doing their work. Working through a reading that illuminates a little piece of what organizes their work settings makes students ready to push further, to see more, and learn more about the everyday exercise of power.

When students grasp the idea of power being embedded in the written materials and in the organizational talk and actions around texts, they begin to reconceptualize what goes on between themselves, their superiors, and their clients. They also reflect differently on contemporary debates, for example, methods for managing public services more efficiently, and about cutbacks in health service funding. They begin to see how people at different sites are tied together to act in concert. The training that this course gives in analyzing the social organization of what they read, and of their own reading, contributes to their development of a new critical stance. They have begun to understand that their own experiences situate them as knowing subjects who can research "what actually happens" to themselves and others.

Chapter Two

Theory "in" Everyday Life

This chapter discusses key concepts and assumptions that support the method of institutional ethnography. Some of these ideas have already been encountered in Chapter One and others will be discussed more fully in later chapters. Here we give primacy to the concepts of social organization, social relations, ruling relations, texts, text-mediation and objective knowing, experience, discourse, and discursive organization – key conceptual tools for thinking about and investigating everyday/everynight life. These concepts, interpreted from Dorothy Smith's usage, express the social ontology that institutional ethnography has been developed to explore. To bring them to life, we are showing how to see them in stories of the everyday. Our objective here is to make the ideas sufficiently understandable to be put into practice.

Social Organization and Social Relations

Institutional ethnographers believe that the world is invariably social and that the only way we can be in the world is as social beings. As Dorothy Smith conceives of it, the social arises in people's activities and through the ongoing and purposeful concerting and coordinating of those activities. Social life is not chaotic but is instead organized to happen as it does. What Smith calls the social relations of everyday life actually organize what goes on. People's own decisions and actions and how they are coordinated with outside events are part of social relations. It is the interplay of social relations, of people's ordinary activities being concerted and coordinated purposefully, that constitutes "social organization."

Institutional ethnography makes use of the forms of social organization that occur routinely in people's lives. These are the forms we take for granted in such mundane activities as buying groceries, borrowing a library book, eating in a restaurant. We also encounter social organization when we engage with the state or large bureaucracies in requesting services or reporting information about ourselves – submitting details of our income to the Tax Department, for example, or our motor vehicle for insurance purposes. The point to understand about socially-organized activities is that we all play a part in generating the phenomena that seem to occur independently.

Everywhere in our daily and nightly lives there is social organization in which we participate without much conscious thought. Smith points out that even our involvement with the physical objects in our world is socially organized. (Smith 1990a, 200). If this seems strange, consider this example: Suppose that, in response to your invitation to "come for morning coffee," a friend arrives at your apartment one morning at about ten o'clock, bringing her young son with her. You welcome the two of them and hang up their jackets. You have already placed the coffee pot and two mugs on the low table that sits in front of your sofa. You and your friend sit down on the sofa and begin to chat about your activities and to drink your coffee. In doing these things, in talking together, in sitting and drinking the coffee as you do at this table at this time of the day, you constitute your activities as a social occasion called morning coffee and the object in front of you as a coffee table. However, your friend's child sees this object with the coffee on it differently. He does not want to have anything to do with what is happening between the two of you. He climbs under the table and tells you it is a house, a house with a strong roof and big, wide windows. He invites you to join him there. What is "coffee table" for you is "house" for him.

While as adults we have the authority to name the table correctly and override his version, in some other situations this would not be the case. Objects become what they are to us by virtue of what we do with them and where, when and with whom they are used. Objects organize our activities in terms of what it is possible to do with them. For instance, at some times of the day your coffee table becomes a footstool as you watch TV or a desk as you prepare your term paper. But it would never work as a bed on which you could stretch out for a nap. The social is constituted in use and in conversation about it. Objects may be accepted as "having" a particular form, but in institutional ethnography, we make the assumption that people constitute them as such. Institutional ethnographers agree with those social theorists who draw back from a belief in the objectivity of things. This social ontology becomes analytically important.

Institutional ethnography makes use of the socially-organized character of everyday life to explore its puzzles. The questions that institutional ethnographers delve into are about how things are socially organized, or put together so that they happen as they do. Analytically, there are two sites of interest – the local setting where life is lived and experienced by actual people and the extra- or trans-local that is outside the boundaries of one's everyday experience. The latter must be investigated in special procedures that allow access to the social organization that extends from elsewhere into people's lives and back outside again. In modern society, texts of all kinds are a ubiquitous feature of social organization and they are accessible to research. Smith coined the term 'textually-mediated social organization' to express the notion that engagement with texts concerts and coordinates the actions of people. The following is an example of textual coordination observed in a local site and offering access to discovery of trans-local activities.

When Fran Gregor lived for a short time in a city in Western Canada, she often rode the bus to the local university. Every day, she observed the same thing: lines of young men and women gathered at bus stops along the route, apparently waiting for the bus. When it came along, they would board one by one, each of them showing a small plastic card to the driver. Some would hold it aloft at the end of an extended arm, others would momentarily flip open their wallet, exposing the card it contained. Each card looked the same. In large letters above a small photo of the person who held the card was the name of the university to which Fran, too, was travelling. The year date was also clearly visible on the face of the card. These symbols Fran interpreted as meaning the cardholders were university students. As each student moved by the driver, he looked at the card and nodded his head. No words were exchanged, each student moved down the bus to a seat, and, after all the passengers had boarded, the bus driver drove to the next stop. The same dance was repeated at each stop along the route. The driver would glance at the card held aloft by each passing student cardholder. Having displayed the card, the student would take a seat on the bus.

This example reveals a commonplace form of textually-mediated social organization. The actions of the bus driver are coordinated with those of the students who first wait for, then board, the bus. Their actions are coordinated with his and take place around the bus pass, which is a piece of text. It authorizes the entry of the student on to the bus to ride apparently without paying a fare. This is an instance like countless others that make up students' daily lives when their actions are coordinated with those of others and a piece of text does the coordinating. Furthermore, this sort of thing happens without much notice on anybody's part because we learn (at least in urban Canada) from a very young age to participate in a textually-organized world. It is only when new forms of text enter our daily lives that we become conscious of textual organization. Consider how the smooth and timely progress of the bus along the route depends on both driver and students acting competently in the situation. Both must understand how to treat the card as relevant to the authority being enacted. The driver plays his part by looking at and acknowledging the propriety of the card. The student's part is to display the card at the very moment she passes by the driver. We can imagine what might happen when a student with no prior experience of this form of access to bus travel enters the bus – explicit instructions would have to be given for the proper compliance to be enacted.

The moment between the bus driver and the student(s), while it displays their actions being concerted through a text, is just the first layer of what there is to know about the social organization of student bus travel in the city. There are all sorts of questions to ask, the answers to which are not obvious to someone watching a student boarding a bus. How does a student acquire the pass? Are all students eligible? On which routes is a pass valid? How is the transit company reimbursed for the travel that the bus pass allows? In asking these questions we are seeking a sense of the complex interweaving of action and text that connects the university, its student enrolment lists, its financial accounting system and so on, to the transit company and its employee practices. For explication of these arrangements, more research would need to be done.

Because of all those questions that are not answerable by simply observing the exchange between the driver and student, we know that university student travel does not begin and end with this routine exchange. If we have the concept "social organization" we are able to use it to recognize that people's actions are coordinated and concerted by something beyond their own motivations and intentions. Using the concept "social relations" is another step in understanding concerted action. Smith proposes that social relations are actual practices and activities through which people's lives are socially organized. Think again of the bus driver and students. The driver looks for the pass; the students display their passes. These are actual actions being carried out by people in real time and an observer can witness this level of activity. But the social relation that is occurring brings in more that that activity. Social relations are *extended* courses of action that take place across social settings. The bus driver and students participate in the social relations but what we witness between driver and student is merely a segment of the social relation that begins elsewhere and continues on after they do their part.

The concept of social relations is being used here as a technical term in institutional ethnography (Smith 1987, 183). Used in this context, it means something different from the way we usually talk about relationships between people – for instance, when referencing the relationship between a teacher and student, or a parent and child. Social relations are not done to people, nor do they just happen to people. Rather, people actively constitute social relations. People participate in social relations, often unknowingly, as they act competently and knowledgeably to concert and coordinate their own actions with professional standards or family expectations or organizational rules. We draw on what we know. This is how we are able to move competently through our days in workplaces or at home, taking up one action after another, in a more or less unselfconscious manner. As competent adults, we know how to get dressed, have breakfast, take a bus, and get to work on time. Or we know how to shop, pay for purchases and get from the mall to our homes, responding to traffic lights correctly and so on. The social relations of this series of actions are invisible, and being part of them does not require the exercise of much, if any, conscious thought. It is only when something goes unaccountably wrong that we stop and notice the organized complexity of our lives that we otherwise navigate so easily.

Smith saw the benefits of being able to make visible *as social relations* the complex practices that coordinate people's actions across separations of time and space, often without their conscious knowledge. This theorizing of connections makes it possible for analysts to explore and clarify what are otherwise mysterious aspects of people's lives. As social analysts, having the concept of social relations makes it possible to recognize and investigate such everyday/everynight puzzles. Social relations may be a conceptualization, but the inquiry it supports is of material things. Something is actually connecting what happens here to what happens there. The analysis shows social relations being realized in people's practices and, as discussed in the next section, in texts.

Texts and the Relations of Ruling

We have been considering how people take up a piece of action and move it forward – by showing a bus pass, for instance. We have made explicit that there is social organization "behind" these seemingly effortless and automatic concerting of actions. Texts are essential to this form of social organization. The organization of social life across geographic sites normally works smoothly because of the proliferation of texts of all kinds and how embedded text-based communication is in social relations. People who have basic literacy skills can go about their daily activities in ways that make a bus pass a useful instrument, or that make a bus schedule "work" as it is written, without ever being aware of the layers of activity that intervene. One actor in a social relation never needs to know the other actors. The text functions to make such invisible connections work.

Smith's approach to understanding texts as components of social relations is enormously useful. It opens up to empirical investigation aspects of power operating in social life that otherwise lie hidden and mysterious. This approach to analyzing texts as part of social relations allows researchers to discover how people are related to each other in pre-determined ways, even if they do not know each other and never even meet. If people handle and process the same texts, they find their actions coordinated by the requirements of working with the text. That is how a text has the power to coordinate and concert – to hold people to acting in particular ways. On the other hand, people who do meet face-to-face and think they are relating to each other as individuals may not recognize how, without their knowing it, their actions are also being shaped by texts. "Ruling" is the concept that Smith uses to name the socially-organized exercise of power that shapes people's actions and their lives. Texts are nearly always implicated in ruling, at least in contemporary societies. Think of how prevalent paper, computers, and information systems are in our own everyday worlds. Texts carry the determinations of many of our actions.

We can see something of the text-based ruling relations in the story told by Jan, the nurse assessor, as it appeared in Chapter One. Text is at the core of Jan's work as an assessor of people who may need some kind of extended health care. The New Brunswick Assessment and Continuing Care Instrument is a text and a constituent of a social relation that Jan participates in with her clients. Jan visits people's homes, asks them questions, and uses her professional judgement about their health status and needs for care. Her questions and observations are guided by the text that she must fill out according to what she learns at her home visit. The categories of the Assessment and Continuing Care Instrument relate to the policies of the provincial government's Department of Health and Community Services concerning the continuing care program. Jan's work makes it possible for the client to be seen through the lens established by the assessment instrument. In interacting with her client through the instrument, Jan is a participant in a text-mediated relation. The instrument is part of a decision process following rules about eligibility and so on. As such, Jan carries a ruling relation into her (helping) interaction with her clients.

However, ruling relations are more than an imposition of rules. They rely on people knowing how to take them up and act in the appropriate manner. Jan's competence is needed in order for this particular ruling relation to work. She has described how she proceeds carefully and skillfully in order to win the consent she needs for the assessment. Note that the social relation between Jan and the client is not theoretical. We hear about how it actually happens – how Jan's conduct of an assessment is regulated through the use of a text can be observed, described, and researched further. The accounts of assessments given by those who do the work will offer some evidence of the actual connection and coordination of different players' involvement in Continuing Care in New Brunswick. To conduct institutional ethnography, we must discover the relations of ruling that texts help to organize and describe the connections across sites that are actually operating.

Activating Texts as Ruling Relations

People routinely conduct their work through texts, forms, and reports. This is particularly true for occupations in the human services where people are processed. Texts are likely to be important and taken for-granted-instruments for the work. Smith talks about texts being *activated* by the people who handle and use them (Smith 1999, 148-51). The notion of activation expresses the human involvement in the capacity of texts to coordinate action and get things done in specific ways. The capacity to rule depends upon carrying messages across sites, coordinating someone's action *here* with someone else's *there*, for instance. An example of activation of a text in a ruling practice draws on a situation somewhat similar to Jan's experience discussed above. Some observational data from a study by Campbell, Copeland, and Tate (1999) show a case manager (a nurse) working within a regional health authority in British Columbia. Like Jan, this nurse also uses an assessment form that is a particular kind of official *text*. Her job is similar to Jan's – it requires her to interview applicants for long-term care services and to gather information about them and their family members and about the health issues that have led to a request for help from a community health program. Here, in an assessment interview, we look more closely at the text-mediated relation being established. Working with the text is the occasion for *activating the assessment form* to establish the applicant's appropriate level of public subsidy for whatever services might be deemed necessary. It turns out this is not a neutral undertaking, but one in which organizational policy and a variety of taken-for-granted assumptions are brought into the helping interaction. In that sense, the activation of the text in question is a procedure both for conducting a health care program and for exercising organizational power.

To speak about this scenario in the theoretical terms we have already introduced, texts and their activation constitute definite forms of social relations between the people involved. Mapping those relations allows analysts to identify how things are organized, how people's lives are ruled. The following excerpt from the transcription of an observed interview shows what kind of relation the activation of the assessment form organized between the case manager and the man who was applying for community health services. Far from being "a servant of the client" – how the nursing case manager understood her relation to her clients – Campbell et al. suggest that this relationship was conducted "in the service of the organization." Moreover, the analysis suggests that the priorities of the organization are very different from those of the applicant for services or even those of any particular case manager. As the assessment interview proceeds, we will see that activation of the assessment form dictates a work process that constitutes a *ruling relation*. We pick up the story as the case manager is interviewing the applicant and has already worked her way through some of the form's categories.

She proceeds to ask questions – the answers to which will provide her with the information that she needs to complete the categories of the assessment form. The text carries an administrative relation that determines what the case manager can be interested in. It makes her act in an unhelpful manner. For instance, the case manager's interest in collecting certain kinds of data means that she does not "hear" the applicant's experiences, including his current state of emotional turmoil about his medical condition and his trouble with pain. The following excerpt offers a glimpse of how this happens:

Case manager: *Can I see that bottle? I'd just like to get the correct spelling and the correct dosage off the bottles.(...) When do you take these... at night?*

Applicant: *One a night, yup.*

Applicant: *I just started that one yesterday, I take one a week...And I take Ibuprofen at night time.*

CM: *Now does this hold the pain for you?*

Applicant: *Not really, um, I just stopped taking that.*

CM: *You've stopped, OK I will not put that down. You're not taking it anymore.*

Applicant: *I do not know, I thought Advil did more for me than these things. See I was taking it for knee pain in the middle of the night, I'm getting pain in the elbows, and knees and hips. I'm getting pain everywhere where there's a joint.*

CM: *Do you smoke?* (Campbell, Copeland, and Tate 1999, 41)

The situation that we glimpse here is of a case manager recording information and following the categories of an agency form. She finishes recording the applicant's medications and moves on to the next category on the assessment form. We are interested in the abrupt change in topic at the end of the excerpt. Here we can see vividly that the assessment form is dictating the flow of her attention. Of course, the form has actually dictated the whole interview, although in a less dramatic way. The applicant has been trying to explain his situation to the case manager. He is in pain and it is poorly controlled by his current medication. He has already explained that he has trouble getting around the house. He is worried about his future and needs information in order to make plans. The case manager is attending to both the applicant's story and to the assessment form's demands for information. She acts both as a professional caregiver – "a servant of the client" – and as a representative of the health care organization that administers the long-term care program.

This example of activating an assessment form allows us to see how her activation work structures the case manager's choices about how to act. The assessment form structures the assessment interview. The form requires that information be collected so that a valid determination of eligibility for public services can be made. The questions that the case manager asks relate to the form's categories, and that is how the organization's interests in determining needs and eligibility, etc. are advanced over any other interests. As you have already come to understand, the social relation of which the applicant and the case manager are part originates outside the room where the interview takes place. The assessment form carries the organizational aspect of the relation into the interaction. No matter how much the case manager hopes to act as the servant of the client, serving the client is not everything that is happening in this interaction. The text organizes this social relation as administrative, making administrative decisions the primary order of business. (As an aside, it should be noted that this is the feature of organizational forms on which management practice depends. Thus we are identifying and speaking not of an aberration, but of established good organizational practice.)

The text-mediation of any professional relationship is a commonplace and normally unquestioned occurrence. Human service provision is routinely organized through records, forms, and reports. Text-mediation regularizes and makes efficient and accountable the delivery of health care, social services, education, and all other human services. As such, it would usually be accepted as not only legitimate but unquestionably of benefit to the client, at least in the long run. But the analysis segment of the assessment interview reviewed here illustrates how contradictions for service provision arise in this commonplace practice. Priorities and interests that are not those of either the health care workers or their clients come to permeate systematically the work of service provision. A text has the capacity to carry a particular idea or meaning across sites and perpetuate it. But to have that effect, people who know how to do so must activate the text. The case manager had the skills, motivation, and authorization to activate the assessment text and to engage with it in the manner that advanced a ruling relation.

Objectified Knowledge and Ruling

Smith uses the notion of ruling as a way of understanding how power is exercised in local settings to accomplish extra-local interests. Ruling takes place when the interests of those who rule dominate the actions of those in local settings. Some forms of knowledge are specialized as technologies for ruling. For instance, in the long-term health care setting being discussed, we saw how the case manager's work made it possible for the information needs of organizational decision making to subordinate the interests of the man who thought he needed services. Smith has written extensively on the importance and ubiquity of text-mediated ruling practices (for example, Smith 1990b, 209-24).

An important shift in knowing occurs when one moves from knowing at first hand to knowing in text-mediated ways. As this case manager worked, she was constructing an objective version of the applicant using a specialized text. It guided her work in a manner that had immediate effects in the setting and as part of a complex organizational process, it would have had extended effects. Here, a ruling practice is being rendered routine, through the use of a text that objectifies the person being acted on, organizationally. Standard questions are asked, categories are filled, and so on. A knowledgeable reader of the assessment form would be able to identify this process and its result as providing the basis for determining eligibility for, and level of, service. What we did not see in that excerpt of data was how this became a ruling practice, although we did begin to form an idea of how the case manager's interest in the client was guided away from the applicant and towards the categories of the form. She is creating a particular description of the client. We can assume that the text organizes her interest towards certain information because some facts are relevant to the organizational decision making and as they are made available there is no further need to address the particulars of the applicant as a person. It is this textual work-up that accomplishes objectification of the client.

Clearly the text-related work of case managers is administratively useful. The goals of administration are coordination and control of the paid effort of employees in the interest of organizational and program objectives. If the text is to work well it must structure the whole interview and subsequent interaction for such organizational purposes. As the example demonstrated, the case manager's interview generated for organizational decision making exactly the information needed to support the decisions that were to be made. On that basis, those decisions could be made not only efficiently, but also equitably and rationally – just as organizational mandates dictate. Besides that, the text of the assessment form created this particular interview as a close copy of other assessment interviews being conducted by other case managers in an administrative area, thus coordinating the effort and attention of all towards the organization's mission.

Institutional ethnographers' theorizing of text-mediated decision making tells them that such decisions will reflect organizational interests that are ruling interests. Even though the categories of the community health assessment form relate to the client's interests – getting help, for instance – that text-mediated process subordinates the client's interests to the organization's. The distinction is fine but vital. As we saw in this excerpt of observational data, the client's interests are transformed into a particular textual version. When the interviewer activates the assessment form, she determines what information "fits" the categories. That selection will appear in and to organizational readers simply as the textual presentation of the client's interests. It creates a version that tells the client's story by removing him as its subject. The objectivity created in this work-up is useful organizationally, especially under conditions where tough decisions have to be made. Agencies face situations where certain apparently eligible applicants have to be screened out on a rational and equitable basis. Categorizing accounts constructs stories into commensurable versions that allow for easier differentiation among people. In situations like this, the interests of people are subordinated.

To clarify this point, we might pursue some of the ways that ruling interests subordinate people's interests in the community health field. The information that a case manager collects makes it possible for her employer to manage scarce resources more effectively, offering services to categories of clients whose needs are more acute, for example. In a health care system like Canada's, acute care is privileged over long-term care through the Canada Health Act and subsequent policy and programs. At issue for the client in the example we have been considering were his plans for managing how to live, increasingly disabled with a degenerative illness. Some health care is publicly provided, while some is not. The objective formulation of his story within the assessment text builds in the policy-relevant categories of information. Let's assume that the categories are there to speak of the acuity of his condition and that the particular decisions about his application for services are to be influenced by the acuity of his needs relative to other applicants.

Even though the professional has constructed it by subordinating the client's story to her views on how to fill out the text's categories, the textual version may appear convincingly objective to her. She will become committed to this version. Smith would call such an account "ideological" owing to the socially-organized practices of its construction (Smith 1990a, 32-45). An ideological account has a ruling conceptual structure that makes it especially useful for organizational decisions. The categories that describe the client express organizational interests — around the questions of how a client's need for service is defined, for example. Case managers may find their own professional views of clients' needs shift as health budgets are tightened to reduce government deficit. When managers must reduce the amount of service provided, cuts can be made, rationally, by considering the texts. People as subjects with individual needs and claims disappear. That is one of the administrative benefits of an objectified account. Case managers become convinced by the apparent objectivity of their textual involvement in the rationing work that an organizational view provides the right way, perhaps even the only fair way, to act. What disappears from their view is the whole question of whose interests are being met and whose interests are being subjugated by a ruling practice. While text-based decisions might appear objective they are not necessarily disinterested or fair.

One of the debates that research in the area of disabilities encourages is about the legitimacy of citizens' claims for long-term health care in a culture that privileges acute care treatments. There is no question that organizational decisions to save money by screening out some clients may favour some over others. Working objectively may not be the right approach. An argument about the influence by proponents of so-called high tech medicine on health policy could be inserted here, for instance, showing that ruling interests can be put in place objectively through administration, policy-making and program implementation.

A shift in conceptualizing the case manager's work from simply conducting an assessment to activating a text-based ruling relation is analytically subtle, but significant. This language identifies how the everyday exercise of power may be identified and studied. And importantly, it introduces the concept of ruling, where ordinarily a health care professional would see this work as being "in the interests of the people." Having a method of inquiry that examines how ruling takes place in routine administrative practices is a very valuable contribution to understanding the troubles that emerge in everyday life. Smith's concept of ruling originates with Marx. However, she names practices of domination and subordination that are specific to contemporary times and not to Marx's (Smith 1990b, 6-8). For example, management practices, for example, of information-based and automated decision processes would not have been available in Marx's time. Smith claims that ruling practices operate and are operated to coordinate us all with the interests of capital in ways that are quite different from Marxist analyses of class oppression in nineteenth-century capitalism. Class and class interests still exist but capitalist business practices, management, and governance have changed, and so have relations of ruling. Texts, language, and expertise of all sorts are now central to the technologies of ruling practices. Technologies for knowing objectively — as illustrated in the community health case — are the basis of contemporary practices of ruling.

While it may not be comfortable for those involved, it is important to recognize that well-intentioned work may be part of oppressive relations of ruling. We can see how this would have been the case in the health care setting examined here. Working within an administratively-framed organization, a nurse's interaction with her clients may be at odds with her own intentions to be caring. People positioned on either side of the relation can participate in ruling practices without their knowledge or consent. Texts and text-mediated practices are central features of this kind of exercise of power. As seen above, the long-term care client becomes, for organizational purposes, the object that the agency account describes. As a subject, he recedes out of sight, while the objectified version carries on into the organization as a "case," a "client," etc. Accounts such as this assessment determine how an organization knows a person, officially, and how the organization's employees can interact with him. The power of an officially mandated organization overrules personal or professional intentions and experiences. In the objectified and ideological version of knowledge being created in organizational records, there is no way back to the client's, or the professional's, own experience. The official objectified version dominates. Any experiential account that the professional makes is neither useful to the organization's action nor likely to be believed. The text replaces and "trumps" competing versions. Officially, the person exists as an object, just as he appears in organizational documents.

Experience, Discourse, and Social Relations

Smith's approach to understanding everyday life and how it is organized and ruled keeps the subject at the centre of the analysis. This is why institutional ethnography is said to begin in personal experience. Maintaining a standpoint in the everyday world offers the institutional ethnographer a stance from which to conduct an inquiry into its social organization. The inquiry is always about how the subject's experience is organized. As discussed above, institutional ethnographers work with a theory of contemporary social organization that is centred on the explication of ruling practices and their associated text-based discourses and objectified forms of knowledge. Here we want to focus on how to see discourse as an organizer of experience while maintaining one's analytic interest in the subject, the knower. DeVault and McCoy trace Smith's attention to the subject in her theorizing of discourse. They distinguish Smith's notion of discourse as used in institutional ethnography from Foucault's use of the term, saying:

> Although [the institutional ethnographic] approach shares with Foucault an interest in texts, power, and governance, there are some central differences that are particularly significant for empirical research. In Foucault's work and in work taking up his approach, for example, the notion of discourse designates a kind of large-scale conversation in and through texts ... For Smith, *discourse* refers to a field of relations that includes not only texts and their intertextual conversation, but the activities of people in actual sites who produce them and use them and take up the conceptual frames they circulate. This notion of discourse never loses the presence of the subject who activates the text in any local moments of its use. (DeVault and McCoy 2002, 772, n. 2)

In Chapter One, we contrasted the narratives of literacy students to the organizational documents they might confront. We introduced a nurse's use of official recording and reporting texts such as a client assessment form The texts of interest to institutional ethnographers are those that are part of institutional or social relationships. These texts, we suggest, are features of discursive organization that relate people purposively to each other, and to events, organizations, and resources. To discover how ideas carried in texts actually affect people's lives, Smith wants us to understand that people *participate* in discursive activity. They participate in discourse as they carry out their everyday lives just as surely as they participate in nutrition and metabolism through eating their meals. What Foucault (1984) conceptualized as knowledge/power is for Smith a social relation that comes into play as actual people participate in knowing and acting knowledgeably. Smith's view is that it is through their active participation and in contributing their own knowledge of how to go about things that people are brought into line with ruling ideas. Some elements of ruling arise formally and explicitly through legally binding discourses. Often ruling happens less explicitly as people consult their own understandings of prevailing and dominant discourses and act accordingly.

A helpful example of discourse as an enacted feature of social organization is found in some research that Smith conducted with Alison Griffith (Griffith 1995; Smith 1987). We have drawn on Griffith's (1995) analysis to illustrate how discourse powerfully organizes mothers' work around their children's schooling and its child-centred ideology. Child-centred teaching focuses on the child in a particular way and to accomplish it, the public school needs the active involvement of mothers. Griffith's interviews with mothers and teachers suggest how more or less easily and successfully mothers take up the work of becoming partners in the educational project (of child-centred education). Schools have come to rely on mothers being ready, willing and able to produce their children as learning-ready and to work along with the teacher in specific ways. Mothers are incorporated into the schooling project through the school personnel's use of ideas (from discourses) about good mothering that all mothers are expected to know and share. Griffith writes:

> A mothering discourse, now taken for granted, is the textual presentation of the dyadic mother-child interaction in terms that have been structured by the child development discourse. It includes (but is not limited to) the advice literature to mothers in magazines and newspapers, portrayals of "good" and "bad" mothers on television and radio, the academic dis-

course on families and the educational literature telling mothers how to improve their child's success at school. (Griffith 1995, 112-14).

Teachers and their teaching processes rely on mothers accepting these responsibilities regarding their child's learning – mothers are expected to work on their children to advance the skills and personal habits that teachers evaluate in the classroom.

Of course, not all mothers in the Smith and Griffith study were equally well-prepared to do this. Some (middle-class mothers) knew the mothering discourses and knew what was required. We can imagine that they may have had college courses in child development, or had attended parenting courses, and they may have kept up with the popular journals that discuss parenting issues. Others mothers, especially working-class mothers, were less familiar with these ideas and what was expected of them. They may also have had fewer resources for working with their children, as Ann Manicom (1995) discovered in her own study of teaching. Manicom's research offers further insight into what this so-called class difference means to teachers and the outcome of their teaching. She showed how teaching that routinely relies on mothering work has better results for the children of families from higher income areas than from lower-income areas. Schools and school districts tend to ignore the real differences between families and between mothers' varying resource conditions for preparing their children for learning and enhancing teachers' work. Her point is that, because of the way that educational resources are allocated across districts, teachers in poorer areas simply cannot teach as effectively. Thus, the policy of relying on mothers' work creates inequities in classrooms. The result of this discourse driven policy is that teaching in inner city schools intensifies the inequality that already exists in society. Manicom's analysis moves responsibility away from individual mothers and teachers and exposes the flaws in policy.

Griffith's (1995) analysis of mothering and schooling gives us some sense of how concepts and theories inform discursive frames that, in turn, have such pervasive effects in people's lives. Families are hooked into schools and educational work through concepts of mothering that are so widely available that schools and policy-makers can routinely rely on mothers to live up to their precepts. Mothers *want* to live up to the school's expectations of them. They tend to *understand* at some level the common perception of what a good mother is and does, even if it asks things of them that they cannot fulfill. The mothering discourse is thus a powerful organizer of people's actions and interrelations. On the one side of the relation are theories and concepts found in educational policies and professional training that guide teachers' work. On the other side are the experiences of the parents – usually the mothers – and of the children who are being educated. In either case, the discourse accomplishes a particular organization of what goes on. In families, it organizes what actually happens in relation to children's homework and other chores, to mothers' attention to children and their television-watching, to supervision, nagging, and so on. Griffith's analysis shows how mothers' relations both to teachers and to their own children are actually organized by how the school expects, and relies on, them to act. There is no explicit authority exercised over mothers, but they learn what they should do. This is what discursive organization of everyday life looks and feels like.

Griffith's study gives one example of how ideas from elsewhere may penetrate daily life, organizing people's relation to their own families, and affecting their everyday choices about how to act with them. What we are calling discourse sets a mother up to feel that either she is, or more often that she is not, doing a good enough job of helping her child succeed in school. The teachers' and schools' structuring of the relations among children, mothers, and teachers relies on mothers accepting the validity of their responsibility. Teachers and schools build authority into this view. There may be some discord, judgement, resentment, anxiety, or guilt in this organization of a mother-child-teacher relation. Yet it is unlikely that someone living the ordinary life of a mother will make the analytic connections that Griffith has done. One's experiential knowledge does not offer insights into discursive organization of everyday life. *Knowing* that the school is downloading educational work on her and that it *requires* her to act in a particular way with her child might bring a mother a sense of relief. But that kind of analysis requires a specialized inquiry.

As its procedure for inquiry, institutional ethnography would not import a theory of schooling and the state into such an analysis. The analysis would rely on a theorized way of exploring power and knowledge – as people's organized activities. The inquiry would attempt to uncover, explore, and describe how people's everyday lives may be organized without their explicit awareness but still with their active involvement. Conceptualizing the operation of power such that it can be discovered in people's everyday actions is a crucial theoretical feature of institutional ethnography. This kind of inquiry begins with a description of what research subjects are actually doing. As in Griffith's work, the analysis brings together an account of people's everyday experiences and actions with a matching exploration of how those experiences and actions are framed through discourses.

Smith's concept of social relations names the sequences of social action that may begin with an individual's activities in local settings but that extend beyond the local, into sites where power is held (see Smith 1990b, 94-5). The concept of social relations also informs a methodological procedure. When the researcher assumes people's actions are undertaken methodically, an inquiry into what happens addresses an actor's (subject's) own procedures. As institutional ethnographers, we know that what the subject is doing is part of the more extended social relation. There will be clues in the informant's account to what informs his actions and where that message comes from. If power enters into what she does, we will need to find out how. In this chapter, we have looked at the coordination of mothers' work with teachers', and earlier, at the interaction of a bus driver and students getting on the bus, and a health care worker with a prospective client. The actions – of teachers, mothers and children, health care workers and clients, or of bus drivers and students – are socially organized. They are coordinated, ruled, put together as part of the social relations of their respective settings. To study these settings means to figure out how each works, how the people we "take the side of" are implicated in social organization that extends beyond them. We have been suggesting how everyday life is discursively organized and how its analysis renders people's lives more understandable. It is possible to discover how the teachers, mothers, health care workers, clients, students and bus drivers involved take up their particular part in a social relation. Theirs is only a piece of the whole. To understand more fully what is happening the researcher must discover and map in the missing pieces of the social relation.

Chapter Three

Beginning an Institutional Ethnography

The day will arrive when it is time to begin a research project. The choice of institutional ethnography as methodology suggests that the beginning institutional ethnographer has gained a certain level of clarity about this approach and what kind of questions it answers. Whether she is a student working towards a thesis, an academic preparing a funding proposal, or a community activist needing to better understand how certain issues are arising, she sees that doing institutional ethnography means taking a particular stance towards the topic. Dorothy Smith has insisted that investigation of the everyday world must begin in a particular orientation of the researcher's interest and attention. Smith talks about entry points for investigation. While this acknowledges her theorized interest in the actualities of people's lives, she is not making a prescription for a particular *sequence* of the research activities. DeVault and McCoy (2002) emphasize this open-ended aspect of the process of inquiry in their paper on interviewing:

> There is no "one way" to conduct an IE [institutional ethnography] investigation; rather, there is an analytic project that can be realized in diverse ways. IE investigations are rarely planned out fully in advance, identifying research sites, informants, texts to analyze, or even questions to pursue with informants. Instead, the process of inquiry is rather like grabbing a ball of string, finding a thread, and then pulling it out; that is why it is difficult to specify in advance exactly what the research will consist of. The researcher knows what she wants to explain, but only step by step does she know who she needs to interview, or what texts and discourses she needs to examine. (DeVault and McCoy 2002, 755)

Yet a beginning institutional ethnographer may benefit from some help to think coherently about a process for conducting the research. Even though there may be more than one correct way of proceeding, there is nothing wrong with having an understanding of where to begin and what to do next. Or, considering all the possible options for research interest in any one setting, it may be helpful to the beginning researcher to learn how to focus on a particular question that institutional ethnography can illuminate. This chapter suggests a possible work process for a beginning institutional ethnographer to follow. It helps her situate herself with respect to a topic so that she can see (in it) a social organization to explore. As one learns about a particular topic, this plan may have to be revised, or even disregarded in favour of some different direction that emerges. It is important to remember that the researcher, like the topic studied, is located in the world around her. In the course of research, useful lines of inquiry may present themselves and, in that moment, may need to be followed up.

This chapter discusses three preliminary preparatory steps for conducting an inquiry in institutional ethnography. The first is to make problematic some feature of the everyday world as an inquiry. Next is to develop a conceptual framework for exploring the problematic. Then we turn to thinking through and writing an account of the methodology that will be used in the inquiry. The discussion offers guidance as to what might be meant by the analytic project of institutional ethnography. It suggests some practical steps one might take to combine theory and methodology in an inquiry that opens up puzzling everyday situations.

Identifying the Problematic of the Research

Institutional ethnographers treat people's lived experiences of the everyday world as the problematic of an investigation. A work process for institutional ethnography begins in, explores, and explicates a particular problematic that is there, being lived by someone, in the everyday world. The notion of problematic also helps the institutional ethnographer identify her own stance in relation to the inquiry – as opposed to methodologically removing herself from it. Identifying a problematic in institutional ethnography requires the researcher to notice and name the relations in the research setting into which she is stepping. One way of distinguishing the relations is for the researcher to write an account of her own knowledge – but one that preserves the voices and actual interactions of those involved – of what happens that contains a puzzling event. This often means doing some preliminary fieldwork – interviews or observations to get the story from those who are living it. The careful writing of that account helps make problematic what is ordinarily taken for granted in the reported experiences – that is, *how* these particular things happen as they do. People's lived experiences are exactly that – lived in the moment and not necessarily thought out; how they happen as they do is likely to remain poorly understood. Even thinking through what is happening or has happened is not the same thing as analysis, of course. To approach an analysis, something troubling in those experiences, or some sense of unease, may suggests a focus or *problematic* of an inquiry.

"Problematic" is a technical term in institutional ethnography, not unlike the range of technical terms used in other analytic approaches. "Constant comparison," "triangulation," and "variable" are technical terms that come to mind and like "problematic" they reference certain activities that are based in their theorized orientations to research. The problematic in institutional ethnography is not the problem that needs to be understood as an informant might tell it, or as a member of an activist group might explain it. It is not the formal research question either. Institutional ethnographers do not study problems as members of settings explain them. Expressions of different theories or explanations that insiders to the setting use might, of course, help a researcher get to a problematic for study. Smith says that she uses the concept of problematic "to direct attention to a possible set of questions that may not have been posed or a set of puzzles that do not yet exist in the form of puzzles but are 'latent' in the actualities of the experienced world" (Smith 1987, 91).

To identify a problematic, you, as researcher, must become familiar with the experienced actualities that Smith talks about. You will decide what to make problematic in a particular research undertaking. Something recommends your focus on a particular puzzle. Think about your topic for institutional ethnography as something that is going on somewhere in the world in which you live. Someone is living the situation that you want to learn more about. It may be that you are living it yourself and know about it personally. It may involve people you know, work with, and care about. Or it may be happening in the life of someone you know about only peripherally. At an early point in your work process you need to learn about your topic, as those who live it know it. You must hear how those who live it talk about it. They are the experts in what is going on at ground level. Theirs are the descriptions you need to consult. This is the way that you begin to identify your research problematic.

The notion of problematic and the work you do to discover the problematic helps you identify the place for inquiry to begin. It also helps you identify your own relation to the inquiry. The identification of the problematic has built into it the notion of a researcher who is committed to knowing on behalf of those whose lives she studies. Identifying what is to be made problematic puts the researcher into the picture as an actor in what is going on. She is now taking the side of potential informants. This may seem to the beginning institutional ethnographer a peculiar idea about the conduct of scholarly research, but it is how institutional ethnographers think about their stance. ("Taking sides" is not entirely new in ethnography; Howard Becker [1967] also used this expression.) For institutional ethnographers it is not just an attitude, it has methodological import, as we discuss below. A set of puzzles arises *for someone*. The world is organized as it is for some purpose. Understanding what is happening makes a difference *to someone*. As people talk about their lives, the researcher begins to identify to whom it makes a difference and why.

Research is always framed from the perspective of those who need to know, whether it is those who are living in the setting or those who are located outside it and looking in. In institutional ethnography, this moment of decision about the problematic is crucial to framing the interests represented in the research. Pursuing scientific objectivity masks this feature of knowledge production, although it does not dispense with it and that is how any research project can be understood as political. In institutional ethnography, unlike some other research, this relation is made explicit. It is not (just) declared. It becomes the basis for how the inquiry is conducted.

The definition of the problematic identifies how the researcher will take up the inquiry from a standpoint in the everyday world. The people who are living the situation that is to be researched know it from inside. Theirs is the moment of recognition that something chafes. Of course, the people involved are not all located in the same way towards what happens. It takes a number of differently located people to enact the event. These coordinated actions generate local experiences that create for those in the setting what Smith calls a disjuncture (Smith 1990b, 83-104). As already suggested in Chapter Two, the issue of disjuncture is between different versions of reality – knowing something from a ruling versus an experiential perspective. As a researcher beginning an institutional ethnography, you must learn about this disjuncture however you can. You may conduct observations or interviews, or engage in casual conversation. If you are drawing on first-hand experiences, you may write up a story about what happened to you. Different people in a situation will have different experiences of it. All such accounts are useful in developing a problematic and should be collected.

The problematic can be understood as a conceptual research tool. Here is how it can be employed. A researcher finds herself in a setting listening to people talk about their lives. In any account of an informant's own experiences there will be important clues about their social organization that the researcher can pick up. These are the entry points to a possible inquiry. They guide the researcher towards a discovery of relevant features of social organization that must be traced and understood to make sense of the setting. The inquiry associated with an institutional ethnography is an investigation of how things actually happen as they do – whatever the people who are involved might make of them. The problematic offers accounts of actual circumstances where actors in the situation participated in its social organization, often unknowingly.

An example may be of use here. Janet Rankin, a PhD student and a nursing instructor, was drawn to study the contemporary organization of nursing work in hospitals when she heard nurses complaining about losing their head nurses in organizational re-structuring. She met with some of these unhappy nurses and listened to their accounts of problems in doing their work, including their theorizing of the problem as "managerial incompetence." As she listened, she heard in the nurses' stories the language of management used easily and as part of the stories about everyday work. Rankin became aware that changes in managerial practices in this hospital included, but were not restricted to, redesign and reallocation of managerial jobs – the issue about head nurses that had sparked her interest in the setting. She began to recognize that the puzzle she would want to explore was "how do hospital nurses integrate (new) managerial efforts and strategies into their own work?" As a problematic, it contained a rupture for those involved between how to accomplish their nursing as the competent professionals they were and how to make the changes in their practice that managerial innovation required. The disjuncture they were experiencing was about the contested definition of "good practice." Rankin's early informants found their work time disrupted. Something was happening in the hospital that created what the nurses experienced as disruption and what hospital management saw as progressive change. The study Rankin undertook was designed to explore the social organization of what she found nurses doing in their everyday/everynight work. She did not focus on people's different perspectives on it, although she did note them. In particular she noted that managers were unaware that anything that they instituted affected nurses' work. Rankin's study focused on the work itself and all the managerial efforts that were going into making the hospital run well and efficiently.

This example illustrates that the purpose of institutional ethnography is to *explore* everyday life, not to *theorize* it. Of course, assumptions about everyday life and how it works reflect the theory on which the research project is based. The Rankin example shows that her choice of how to establish a problematic for study relied on her belief that social life is socially organized and that it would be interesting and useful to discover and describe the socially-organized features of the setting, including how ruling practices are involved. She was already working with a theorized view of health care, hospitals, nursing and so on, which positioned her to hear the nurses' stories in a particular way. It focuses attention on social relations, as opposed to individual actions and competence. This is an important point for beginning institutional ethnographers to catch as significant. *A problematic for inquiry can emerge for a researcher only when the particular theoretical framework of institutional ethnography is used.* Previous chapters have offered the basics of this theory. A great deal more writing on the subject is available for those who want to dig deeper.[7]

The Conceptual Frame for a Research Project

A review of relevant literature is the basis for analysis and critique of what is already known about events of the kind that the researcher is exploring. The above example of Janet Rankin developing a problematic for study suggested that she had learned how to position herself as an institutional ethnographer in the setting. At first, she addressed herself to the issues the nurses were worried about in the same way that they did. She learned from them how they were involved. She heard what was actually happening from their perspective. She accepted their accounts as true – after all they were living these experiences. Then, as institutional ethnographer, she had to learn to see things differently. Not only must she learn to think, hear and talk about the setting as various participants in it know it, but she must also attend to institutional ethnography's interests in how a setting is organized. She positioned herself through knowing the setting in a certain theorized way. She had made herself ready to explore the social relations of the nurses' experiences even before she entered the setting as a researcher. When she began to understand the nurses' points of view, she found that she needed more information on the specifics of the managerial efforts to restructure the hospital. She found a vast literature on this.

How does an institutional ethnographer make use of the literature? A demonstration of the background of a project is a required feature of most research proposals. Reviewing the literature helps researchers reflect on different kinds of knowing about their topic and how their own research would add to what is already known. Whether a researcher is writing a funding proposal, a thesis proposal or the thesis itself, a research project must be linked to the scholarly literature. Researchers want to discover what is already known about a topic and how their take on an issue relates to what others have said. This is true for any scholarly undertaking. It is a requirement in scholarly research to hook new knowledge to the discourse in which the topic is already known. Thesis writers must demonstrate their skill in becoming part of this scholarly tradition as part of the test of their competence. Funding proposals are evaluated partly on how adequately new work takes up ideas that have already met the tests of scholarship. Usually, the development of a literature review is a time-consuming activity for the researcher but is otherwise not troublesome. Libraries offer help with the technology of doing literature searches.

A few more words need to be said about the stance that the institutional ethnographer takes towards the literature. This institutional ethnographer's reading is contrasted to the literature review that is usually required in a thesis. In institutional ethnography, the researcher reads the literature both for conventional reasons – to discover the scope of research knowledge in this area – and for a particular reason related to her own positioning. The institutional ethnographer's research stance maintains the research interest in the social organization of the topic. For the beginning institutional ethnographer, the work of conceptual framing of the research project identifies both what is known and what needs to be discovered about the topic to explicate its social organization. A conceptual framework helps the researcher focus on those aspects of the puzzle that the inquiry must address. It also begins to show how the issue of knowing emerges as a contested aspect of research – that, in institutional ethnography, is made explicit.

Making use of the literature in institutional ethnography helps establish the researcher's position in the research. It requires a different way of reviewing the literature that institutional ethnographers must learn to do. The contested terrain of knowing is an enormously important issue and it hits the beginning researcher the moment she begins to read the literature. She must come to terms with the literature while delineating and maintaining her particular stance *vis à vis* discourses, authorized knowledge, and views that express a standpoint organized differently from the institutional ethnographer's stance in the everyday world. Dorothy Smith's development of institutional ethnography took place in the context of her own realization that scholarship had alienated and oppressed some people, including women. Using the oppressors' language is still dangerous and the achievement of institutional ethnography is to offer methods whereby oppressions can be explored and understood. That said, one's first commitment as an institutional ethnographer is to an investigation of "what actually happens" as those who live it experience and talk about it. The literature may speak about the topic one way, while the people on the ground will speak about it another. As already suggested, scholars usually treat research accounts as authoritative. However, when an institutional ethnographer reads the literature, it is not just for the facts, but to analyze the literature's social organization. As she does this kind of reading, the institutional ethnographer must remember that what she reads has been generated in research activities that have mainly disappeared from the accounts on library shelves. Institutional ethnographers remain interested in how those accounts have been constructed as factual and in how facticity depends upon the research-writers' standpoint disappearing from the final version.

The danger in reading the literature and in beginning to use the concepts of these studies to think about one's own topic is the possibility of importing dominant perspectives into one's own thinking about the research setting. Much of this book, so far, has been about the usefulness of beginning in the everyday world and in the experiences of people who inhabit it. It is they who bring it into being as it is. We have emphasized how the goal of this approach is to make the world understandable for those with whom the researcher stands. The danger inherent in importing concepts from the literature into the descriptions of the topic is that one usually cannot see how such concepts carry with them a particular positioning of the reader. All research writing situates both the researcher (writer) and the reader (Smith 1990). Unless you, as institutional ethnographer, self-consciously attend to your own research stance, you may leave behind the problematic of the everyday world, subordinating it to the interests and stance built into the literature. Were you to do so you would find yourself standing with the view of the world (and of research subjects) that is represented in the literature. You would have lost your stance in the everyday world.

Scholarship is conventionally conducted to generate *objective* knowledge, as if the researcher were positionless. This has been the standard remedy to the problem of bias as it plagues research done in naturalist or positivist modes. Conversely, some other researchers may be seeking and attempting to represent research subjects' own views. This kind of research is explicitly interested in discovery and presentation of the subjective understandings (of informants). Institutional ethnographers do neither. We discussed earlier how the adequacy of research findings in institutional ethnography depends upon establishing for readers the position from which the account is written. Institutional ethnographers believe that where the knower stands determines what can be seen. This is a theorized approach that makes reviewing the literature a special kind of undertaking for institutional ethnographers. Institutional ethnographers often find themselves reading to identify how the researcher-writer is located, the purposes for which a particular account is written and what activities this particular account supports – or, alternately, makes invisible.

Here is an illustration of how reading the literature may be problematic for an institutional ethnographer. A graduate student, Sonya Jakubec, reflects on her experiences as a mental health worker in Africa. She reads the literature published by the World Health Organization and written by health care analysts who routinely conduct research for international organizations. She discovers that these studies in the mental health literature use concepts such as "burden of disease." While this concept is central to the collection of statistics in her area of research, it becomes clear to her that this formulation carries with it assumptions that come from the work of administering international aid. Knowledge of health in developing countries is worked up in health research conducted by researchers from developed countries and relates to (that is, makes possible) certain kinds of decisions about aid programs and their funding and evaluation. Jakubec tapped into a discourse of international development, policy and health that frames how international agencies "see" developing countries. If she were to adopt the concepts of this discourse to understand her own topic she would find herself taking the standpoint of the agencies, regardless of her own intent. To maintain her interest in understanding what is happening on the ground where she used to work, it may help her to recognize that when funding decisions are made, funders think about a setting as having a "burden of illness" quotient. That too becomes important data for Jakubec's analysis. However, if she imported that concept into her own inquiry, she would begin to see the everyday world from a dominant perspective. She would find that what she and her co-workers knew and worried about in their everyday lives in Africa would be translated into concepts that would not allow them to speak about what was important to them, as insiders to the local setting. The relevancies of international development would overwrite and overwhelm what was actually happening in the local setting.

As an institutional ethnographer writing a conceptual framework, you are delineating your own research stance in contrast to those you find in the literature. This is in itself a theoretically-orientated undertaking. Its success depends upon you, the researcher, having grasped how all research and knowing are activities that are located (because, according to the theory, all researchers are always located somewhere). Sonya Jakubec's study needed to be located in relation to her experiences of working in a particular place (see Chapter Six). She recognized that her interests were different from the interests of those who were planning and delivering international aid. Understanding what other scholars have already said about her topic helped her better understand her own problematic. As she considered how others had seen her topic, how they have explored it from different angles and perspectives, she gained a clearer picture of what she must explicate by further research. Like Jakubec, any institutional ethnographer will be getting some insight into the relevant discourses and how her own experiences and interests situate her in relation to, and differently from, them. Working this out is one of the tasks of writing a conceptual framework. It brings the institutional ethnographer to increased clarity about the focus of her own inquiry in the everyday world, in contrast to the already published studies that she analyzes.

Writing an Account of the Methodology

An account of the methodology to be employed is usually required for a scholarly research proposal and is always part of a thesis. Later, after the analysis is written, the write-up must include a detailed description of the study and how it was conducted. The two accounts will be somewhat different. A careful preliminary write-up of the methodology helps students to think through in advance how research questions are answered in institutional ethnography. This, in turn, helps them think about what kind of data they will need and alerts them to consider how they will get access to it. In proposals, researchers may be expected to address questions of the knowledge claims they will make, including how the findings of their study might be generalized, under what circumstances their findings will be trustworthy, and the more technical questions of how they will collect relevant data. In retrospective descriptions, readers expect to see a step-by-step account of exactly what happened.

An adequate explanation of methodology satisfies readers — whether they are a peer review committee, an expert panel, or a thesis supervisory committee, and eventually an external examiner — that the research follows accepted procedures within the relevant scholarly community. That suggests that the researcher must familiarize herself with the external standards that the account of the methodology must meet. What scholarly community is relevant to one's research? What are its important methodological debates? If you are working in institutional ethnography, you might need to speak about how it conforms – or not – to the standards of qualitative research, for instance. Your own academic discipline may have expectations for research that you must meet. Or you may at least want to demonstrate that you know what they are. Besides addressing the relevant scholarly community, the methodology section of a proposal is also concerned with internal research criteria. For instance, when the research design and methods of data collection and analysis are described, they must appear consistent with the statement of research methodology. Another element of the internal criteria of adequacy appears in the write-up of the research where competent readers must be able to see for themselves that the methodology has been realized. Competent readers will judge the status of conclusions you have drawn from your analysis in relation to your prior explanations of the methodology. In other words, the statement of methodology is there to allow readers to make the same sense of the analysis that the researcher is making. Researchers must do what they have said in their account of their methodology. It offers readers instructions on how to read the analysis. It must say the right things and be comprehensible. The scientific nature or validity of research results is established when methodical procedures are logically consistent with an accepted and adequately described theory of knowing and are demonstrably followed.

Exactly what detail is required in a methodology section of a proposal depends upon convention or explicit instructions. Students can consult completed theses in their faculties to see what is conventionally expected of them. Researchers applying to a funding agency or program will get some indication of the requirements from the published guidelines and categories of the application forms. New researchers should consult more experienced colleagues who have been successful in the grant competitions that they are entering. Institutional ethnographers may be expected to offer more comprehensive explanations of their methodology than researchers employing more conventional research approaches. Just how much explanation is deemed adequate will often depend upon the expertise of the readers of the proposal or the research report. So research writers should ask themselves "what, if any, prior knowledge of institutional ethnography do the intended readers have?" It would be highly unusual, for instance, to expect a survey researcher to explain probability theory in order to rationalize her decisions about sampling. A certain level of knowledge of this kind of research can be presupposed in any panel of reviewers – certain conventions become accepted knowledge in research. Just as scientific equipment for measuring samples of fluids in neurophysiological research embodies taken-for-granted theory (Latour and Woolgar 1979, 66), so too are certain theories embedded in the routine technologies of social research. Many social science routines and research practices (testing a hypothesis, sampling) are also taken for granted. Any technique may acquire the status of being commonly accepted over time but until this happens, researchers who use approaches that rely on theories of knowing that are new or alternative are expected to explain their practices in more detail. That may put extra demands on the writing of methodology by institutional ethnographers. We usually have to explain our practices as *exceptions* to commonly understood techniques.

A solid explanation of methodology helps the institutional ethnographers avoid the unfortunate situation of having to answer for every deviation of their research activities from the practices of conventional ethnographers. And there are many such differences in how an institutional ethnographer goes about her work. Producing an account of the research to be reviewed by university ethics committees may therefore be difficult even though the ethical considerations are impeccable. One methodological difference that becomes a problem relates to the demand to produce the interview schedule as part of an ethics review. What ethics reviewers expect in a researcher's standard account of their design and plan, including questions to be asked in interviews, emerge *out of* the research process for institutional ethnographers, rather than being determined at the outset. Even the choice of informants is determined by the course of the inquiry rather than by a pre-determined plan. It must be this way to be true to this approach. As one aspect of the problematic is explored, the researcher gains new insights that point to who knows best how this all works. Her task is to follow that lead. It stands to reason that the questions one would ask of a newly designated informant also emerge as the inquiry proceeds and the researcher's knowledge grows. The research process follows the shape of the problematic in the everyday world that the researcher explicates, not the shape of a plan developed prior to undertaking the inquiry.

In discussing the kind of problems this approach to research offers ethics committees, and subsequently for applications from institutional ethnographers, Timothy Diamond (2001, personal communication) draws attention to the role of institutional ethics committees and their mandates. Diamond's own research

(1992) in a U.S. nursing home taught him valuable lessons in negotiating access and negotiating with ethics committees. In his consideration of these issues, he uses the language and theory of institutional ethnography saying that the work of ethics committees is itself text-based, activating certain protections within certain ruling relations. While these may in some cases protect research subjects, this would not be their only or primary purpose. Rather, ethical review procedures protect corporations from litigation, for instance. Diamond proposes that university procedures for reviewing the ethics of research projects have trouble with applications from institutional ethnographers partly because this research does not study people as such. Instead, it studies activities and how they are organized, and relations often crystallized in texts. Thus, the abstract subject of ethical concern to a reviewer is not the subject of an institutional ethnography. Indeed, there may be no subject of the research in the sense that ethics committees conceptualize the human subjects of research. Sometimes, to expedite approval from an ethics committee, the researcher has to generate a virtual subject to fulfill the expectations of the ethics committee.

Up until now, this section on writing an account of the methodology has focused on what can be written at the proposal stage. Of course, the study must also be described after the data collection has been completed. Writing up the study and its methodology is part of doing the analysis and a description of what was actually done will differ from the prospective account of the research design and plan. For thesis writers, this means going back to the proposal's account of your methodology and altering it. You remember what you did and its sequencing. You consult your notes and you may notice that you want to include things in the account of the study that you would not have considered part of the research before. Or you may need to edit out those elements of your plan that did not materialize, at least not in the manner you had expected. This may need explanation. You may also find that you actually relied on some event or learning that directed your attention in a certain manner. For instance, when Sonya Jakubec went to write up her study, she recalled things that, prior to doing her analysis, had not seemed important. One example of this was remembering that the international aid agencies she approached for funding sent her to search out authorized approaches to describing her mental health team's needs for resources. Previously she had talked about being frustrated by the demands for more and better information. Now she recognized that the agencies knew what they wanted in terms of information about the field. Yet this was not how they had spoken to her about the information they required. For them, the information was either good enough or not good enough to support a request for funding. As Jakubec's analysis proceeded, this point about the social organization of knowledge of mental health became understandable to her. Being instructed to use a particular authorized form for recording local needs had quite simply not seemed significant before. The analytic work that made sense of that piece of "what actually happened" brought it forward as something to mention in her retrospective write-up of her study.

The retrospective writing about the study allows you to speak with confidence about its time frame, what worked and what did not, and how you solved problems of data collection. The study is often a sub-headed section of your methodology where you relate the process of data collection. In this sub-section, you will introduce the informants, situate them, and give readers all the details that they will need to feel at home with your study when they turn to your analytic chapters.

Chapter Four

Collecting Data for an Institutional Ethnography

Possibly nothing is more important to data collection than a good grasp of what institutional ethnography can do and how it does it. The emphasis in the preceding chapters has been on developing, explaining, and theorizing institutional ethnography's distinctive focus for research. We have emphasized that, before attempting to gather data for an institutional ethnography, the researcher needs to learn how to look at any situation *as an institutional ethnographer does*. Institutional ethnographers bring a particular interest to studying social settings and interaction in everyday life. They are interested in the particular conditions under which experiences arise and are lived *by someone*. And although this person is not actually studied, the specialized investigation undertaken does keep the subject at its centre. The inquiry is always about circumstances located in the world of the subject, even if it is outside the subject's experience and knowledge. And that has implications for the data collection.

Explicating Ruling Relations

Institutional ethnographers explore a particular problematic in explicating what is happening in a local setting, as people know and live it there. The notion of explication is important – it is the analytic core of the research process in institutional ethnography. We say that researchers begin in the everyday world, collect data about it, and proceed to explicate a problematic by going beyond what can be known in any local setting. There are really two levels of data and data collection involved in explication. Data collection has to expand beyond what people in the local setting know and do. There is always something missing from even very good experiential accounts made by people who live the events in questions. Some aspects of their lives are organized outside what they can know about from being there in the everyday world of experience. Outside forces – people, events, diverse forms of organization – affect them but do so more or less invisibly. To understand the workings of any setting involves learning how people, seemingly positioned outside the setting, are nevertheless active inside it. In Chapter One, we saw Jan reflecting on her assessment work and seeing how decisions external to her own judgement affected what happened to her clients. A bit of digging turned up evidence of organized courses of action that could account for her experiences.

The two levels of data that are needed for analysis in institutional ethnography appear in Chapter One's presentation of Jan's situation. While talking about doing Continuing Care assessments, Jan speaks of something that actually happened in a work setting. A researcher in the setting might take down her story in a field note. A field note about Jan's work is entry-level data because it offers an entry into a problematic in the everyday world. Whatever happened that Jan talks about was organized somehow and an inquiry can discover how things happened that way. Entry-level data is about the local setting, the individuals that interact there and their experiences. The research goal is to explicate that account. Some more research must be done and some more data collected. Depending on what question is deemed interesting, the researcher might interview other assessors and clients of Continuing Care, to learn more about local conditions and experiences. The researcher must verify that the original story was not idiosyncratic. Others in the same, or similar, settings will have their own stories that relate to Jan's experiences in some way. While we would not expect their experiences to be the same as Jan's, they will be about a similarly organized phenomenon. With the problematic emerging, the next step is to go looking for data that will explicate it – what we are calling level-two data. How to find level- two data has also been suggested in Jan's account in Chapter One. Some detective work must be done to discover the missing organizational details of how the setting works. It calls for field research – not about Jan, other assessors, and their involvement with clients, but about the broader setting. Perhaps there are some documents about the working of the Continuing Care program that will be useful. The two levels of data are connected, of course. Indeed, Jan's story offers methodologically important clues for the researcher to follow towards the collection of data useful for the explication. The researcher will recognize useful data when they illuminate her original story about Jan and her concerns.

The theory upon which institutional ethnography relies tells us that the settings that we investigate are organized and ruled in definite ways, albeit in ways that are often not fully understood by participants. Inquiries are conducted into such questions as "what are the connections across and beyond the boundaries of this setting and how are they enacted by actual people?" As Chapter Two proposes, the purpose of establishing such linkages is to explicate relations of ruling. This kind of inquiry makes power understandable in terms of relations between people, relations that rule. Institutional ethnography's focus on explicating ruling relations gives this scholarly research its potential for being a resource for activism and for transformation of the conditions of people's lives. Learning how people's lives are organized outside their own knowledge and control makes it possible to understand domination and subordination. DeVault and McCoy say that the analysis produced "is like a 'map' that can serve as a guide through a complex ruling apparatus" (DeVault and McCoy 2002, p.754).

The theory that we have been outlining in earlier chapters directs a researcher's attention to the kind of data needed for a particular inquiry – where the goal is always explication of how everyday life is put together. Many studies in institutional ethnography begin with fieldwork and rely on observational methods, interviews, and documents to help establish a problematic for study. The data for explication are collected using the same range of methods. Because the topics that interest institutional ethnographers are as varied as the activities of everyday life itself, the data-collection methods are basically whatever makes those topics available for analysis. While some institutional ethnographers use the whole range of data types and data-collection techniques available, others may use the institutional ethnographic approach to focus on quite narrow data sources, such as autobiographical or textual data.

Positioning Oneself as a Researcher: Research Relations

When data collection is being planned, institutional ethnographers must give careful consideration to the relations of research they are entering. There are people to meet and talk to about the research plan. There are formal relations to be negotiated consisting of issues of access – permissions, approvals, ethical reviews, and organizational and individual consents. We have already discussed some questions about ethics and ethical reviews of institutional ethnography in Chapter Three. While the formal issues of access tend to be treated and written about as part of one's research methodology, we want to discuss them here as the relations of research. For instance, it may be useful for the researcher to recognize the relation she participates in as she prepares her application for ethics approval by the university's ethics committee. She is entering a relation of ruling in which she is a supplicant. Rules established (in Canada) by the Research Tri-Council govern any university's requirements of an individual researcher. The researcher must organize and represent her research plans in a manner that coincides with these requirements – whether or not the categories and criteria of the particular forms are relevant and appropriate to her study. A university's ethics committee becomes an authority that uses those rules to interpret an application and determine whether or not the research plan is approved. Established in the interests of ensuring ethical research behaviour, the rules are applied as an administrative matter – filling forms adequately, matching words to categories, etc. For the researcher, success in passing the ethical review means learning how to position oneself and one's research within the frame of relevance that is organizationally established. As discussed in Chapter Three, the ruling concerns of universities and committees can have an impact on the original concerns about ethical research. A number of related matters intervene. For instance, university prestige is linked to attracting funds and to opportunities for the commercialization of its research successes. But along with that come increased fears of litigation and the overriding attention of ethics reviewers to legal issues. All this can distort the realm of ethical reviews. Institutional ethnography fits uneasily into this administrative domain for a number of reasons, but primarily because of its interests in producing knowledge for people, in contrast to knowledge for ruling.

It may be that, at the same time as the university ethics review is proceeding, the institutional ethnographer is also negotiating access to an organization where some or all of the research will be conducted. Winning organizational approval may be particularly challenging for an institutional ethnography owing to the kind of data that are sought. As a researcher, before you approach an organization to secure their cooperation in a study that involves their employees, activities and work processes, clients, etc., you must begin to conceptualize the relations into which you are entering. This process of seeking permission, like the university's review, may be called an "ethics review," but community organizations have their own issues about approving research within their walls and practices. As a researcher, you may be enthusiastic about the value of the work you intend to do and its scholarly potential. Yet, participating or cooperating in your research may or may not be perceived as beneficial to the organization. Receiving ethical approval from the university for your study may not satisfy the community organization either. Organizational leaders may see various kinds of drawbacks to opening elements of their operations to a researcher's, and thus to public, scrutiny. Government agencies may offer special difficulties – governments have clear rules about employee confidentiality because they operate in a highly political environment. Private firms may maintain secrecy about their products, production processes, and sales in order to maintain their competitive edge in the market place. (This also applies to profit-making companies that offer human services.) Public service institutions, besides protecting their clients' privacy, may be hesitant to cooperate with research, fearing its intrusion into a work process aimed at efficient use of workers' time. Labour relations sometimes create obstacles to openness in organizations where circulation of certain information might compromise bargaining positions, etc. When organizations express reluctance to cooperate with research, they are likely to mention these kinds of reasons.

In addition to the above, researchers need to be aware that organizations typically exercise caution about disclosing organizational information. Information is frequently thought of as an organizational resource that should be managed for maximum benefit. Reluctance to share it may have something to do with how an organization's work constructs insiders and outsiders, hierarchies of knowers, through the distinctive use of language, systems, records, procedures and practices.[8] Outsiders may misunderstand processes, texts and language that are particular to an organization and this could be embarrassing to the organization in various ways. Routines constructed in relation to internal language and texts may maintain the organization's influence over the activities of its constituents and streamline its work processes; or they may generate loyalty and a positive public image, etc. Research that has not been commissioned by the organization and is not under its control may be seen as potentially disruptive of the smooth operation that is aimed at. Institutional ethnography, because of its goal of taking a standpoint outside a ruling position, is not likely to be conducted as an internal research project. It is more likely to explore and critically analyze some aspect or activity of the organization.

The benefits of having an institutional ethnography conducted in an organization may not be easy for a beginning researcher to explain to its executives. Of course, there are good reasons for doing this kind of research, including benefits to the organization, and these good reasons can be conceptualized and described.

To do so, the institutional ethnographer, in working up her description of the research project and plans, needs to take seriously the real-world conditions in which the organization exists. She needs to consider the problems – routine or otherwise – with which its leaders are confronted. It will help the researcher's case if she is able to represent the benefits of the study in terms that make sense of these problems. If the researcher can conceptualize how her study opens up such problems to better understanding, then she clearly stands a better chance of gaining the cooperation she needs to conduct the research. Given that understanding the standpoint of clients or employees is an element of any successful organization, and of strategies for improvement of its operations, the kind of knowledge gained by institutional ethnographers should be seen as beneficial. Yet, there are significant challenges in explaining that to organizations.

The difficulties are compounded by the methodology that makes the practical conduct of institutional ethnography hard to explain. As Chapter Three suggested, an inquiry in institutional ethnography is not neatly packaged and its parameters clearly bounded as with some other types of research. According to DeVault and McCoy, "(Institutional ethnographers) know what they want to explain, but only step by step can they discover whom they need to interview, and what texts or discourses they need to examine" (DeVault and McCoy 2002, 755). Because institutional ethnography seeks answers to everyday issues of how things work, it is likely to expand its inquiry into organizational action and move into uncharted territory as the natural course of the inquiry is followed. It thus offers the potential to explore and disclose issues that organizational leaders may not fully understand. This can be threatening if an organizational leader is not prepared to see things – including elements of his own position – in a new light. The issue of access often comes down to the trust that a researcher and organizational representative can establish and whether they can have a meeting of minds on the importance of the research goals.

Besides convincing organizational leaders to cooperate with the research, researchers must interest ordinary members in acting as informants. How the people in research settings feel about being part of a study will vary and this can influence how easy or difficult a research project will be to conduct. The people inhabiting the settings you are studying are the source of much important knowledge. If they are keen to work with you, your research will go much more smoothly than if they are not. People may be supportive of your study or they may be reticent about it and about being involved. Learning how to explain the research in ways that allow organizational personnel to see it as interesting to them, and something they want to support, is yet another aspect of your research. Having formal support from informants' supervisors is the foundation and it allows a researcher to request the involvement of volunteer informants. But there are potential drawbacks in being seen as sponsored by upper management. People on the inside of organizations may not all share the views of the leadership and that may affect a researcher's relationships with potential informants.

Managers are likely to see themselves as having a broad overview of the organization while they think that their staff has a narrower view, one that comes from being located in a particular department or position. Besides a broad or a narrow perspective, this might also be talked about as having, or not having, a management perspective. Institutional ethnography proposes a somewhat different way to think of differing perspectives. We have been explaining that institutional ethnography assumes a particular social ontology, where different actors constitute a setting as it appears and is lived. In this view, each participant is located in the social relations of the setting, but positioned differently. Each person will know the setting from participating differently in its social relations and will therefore each have their own organized standpoint. How different participants understand the setting, their work, etc., will not therefore necessarily coincide. Nor will informants who are lower-level workers see the research in the same way as members of the organization who are located in upper-level positions. But the notion of standpoint moves away from acceptance of a managerial perspective as correct or more adequate, even though it has that status within the organization. This is an important analytic point for researchers. It may also help, when they attempt to represent their research interests to various organizational groups, to remind themselves of their audience's standpoint.

Regarding ethical reviews, people with the authority to give approval and to agree to make information available may expect to see and hear certain kinds of descriptions of the proposed research activities. Those expectations may not match the work process that an institutional ethnographer undertakes. It is always a challenge for the researcher to be able to recognize at the time that initial research cooperation is being negotiated that there are different kinds of interests at play in a setting. It calls for careful preparation of presentations aimed at getting cooperation. Understanding different standpoints comes from theorizing the inquiry as institutional ethnography and it also requires a solid work-up of the "real-world" area of study prior to entry into a setting. This may feel like a classic Catch 22 situation – some of the research must be done before one can feel properly prepared to seek access to the research site.

While access to an organization will depend on upper-level support, the study's success depends just as heavily on the development of good relations between informants and researchers. Many things can go wrong at the data-collection phase but, on the other hand, informants more often than not find that being involved in the research is interesting and even useful to them and to their work. The theory of institutional ethnography offers the basis for the best strategy for involving local participants. In institutional ethnography, informants are understood to be experts in what they do. Researchers rely on learning from them. Working with each individual informant offers the researcher an opportunity to explain this research stance to potential informants. An explanation of how the researcher understands the status of someone's expertise often helps to reduce the anxiety that informants may otherwise feel about answering questions. Once they grasp that the researcher actually means it when they say "you are the expert here," the informant will no longer have to worry about not knowing the answers to research questions.

Another source of reluctance to be involved comes from the potential informants' concern about the researcher's relationships with the organizational leadership. While the consent form will address confidentiality, it may not reassure informants thoroughly about the purposes of the research. They may be skeptical. Members of big organizations are learning that methods of management and organizational change often include a research phase and have negative consequences that affect them down the line. Unless a trusting relation with a researcher is developed, workers may feel they are coming under a form of managerial surveillance and may wonder if everything they say is somehow going to be used against them. Researchers must be careful to avoid developing deals with organizational leaders that compromise their relations with informants.

More about Data Collection and Interpersonal Relations with Informants

The preceding section addressed issues of power that permeate research settings, especially those that are part of large organizations. A related concern is about the power of the researcher. Critique by those who have consistently been the object of research rather than in charge of doing it has problematized the interpersonal research relation. Feminist researchers have argued that researchers bring power into research settings, and how that is dealt with is an important feature of data collection and of the whole research enterprise. This is a serious issue in data collection and needs to be treated as such by any researcher.

First, let us consider the interpersonal relation that is established between the institutional ethnographer and the people they interview or observe. Like other ethnographers, institutional ethnographers may speak of the people in the settings they study as informants. That is one term that we too have been using in this book. Sometimes we use different terms – for instance, we may talk about observing someone who is a participant or an actor in the setting we are studying. Some researchers feel that the term chosen signifies something about the research relation and, more especially, how its power is distributed. Of course, the choice of a particular term does not itself alter the nature of the relations involved but the nature of the research relation is contentious enough among researchers to bear some more discussion here. Feminists have recommended ways to establish research relations that are equitable and not exploitative (Reinhartz 1992; Roberts 1981). In the introduction to the second edition of their book on feminist methods, Stanley and Wise say that, in making efforts to reduce the psychological distance between the researcher and whoever is being observed or interviewed, feminists proclaim the egalitarian impulse in their research. But they do admit that academic social science done by feminists has continued to create a hierarchy between "'us,' the theorizing researching elite (feminists) and 'them,' the experiencing researched (women)" (Stanley and Wise 1993, 7). The problem of power relations in research has yet to be solved by feminist methods.

Researchers working within the various approaches to participatory research also work from principled positions about power relations in research (Gaventa 1988; Hall 1992). For practitioners of Participatory Action Research, the issue of who has the power to define a research problem, to determine how it should be studied, and ultimately to interpret the findings and act on them, is so important that research participants themselves must take control of it (Cocks and Cockram 1995; Park 1992). Such a perspective revolutionizes research by transferring research decision making and control away from scholars and into the hands of those who want their concerns studied. Participatory research is often considered to be an activist undertaking and part of a struggle waged by people who are seeking more power in their lives. It is probably important to recognize that institutional ethnography attempts something different from most participatory research. For institutional ethnographers, the conceptualization of power as ruling is decisive for how the inquiry is taken up. Institutional ethnography even problematizes some of the central assumptions of participatory research. Consider, for instance, the participatory research that was conducted as an institutional ethnography and reported by Campbell, Copeland, and Tate (1998; 1999; see also Chapter Six, this volume). This paper argues that participation is itself not an answer to the exercise of power in research and that being participatory does not necessarily equalize research relations. However, they concede that when one is attempting to build knowledge from the standpoint of a person or group and to build knowledge for them as does institutional ethnography, the inquiry must attend to interpersonal interactions, too. Campbell et al. (1998) concluded that the notions they brought into the research about equalizing research relations through participation may have been "an ideological construct and not an achievable goal" (100). Here is what they say about that:

> The ideal of equality that the staff carried into the research is being reconceptualized over the course of the project. We are no less committed to participation but are learning to see it as a practical activity that does not put it outside the ruling relations of research. "Participation" as such does not prevent staff from exercising power, nor does it necessarily ensure that the research addresses the needs of the researched. Participation, we argue, must be understood within a research framework that addresses power as enacted in everyday life. Then, decisions that support participation can be undertaken within the range and complexity of other research relations and responsibilities. (102)

Institutional ethnographers agree that the question of power is important to researchers, to those who are the subject of research, and to how research knowledge is used. We are particularly aware that the production of knowledge is itself integral to relations of ruling and to the exercise of power in official, and perhaps even unofficial, ways. The radical potential of institutional ethnography is to rethink social settings taking existing power relations into account. Institutional ethnography is theorized and its research design developed in such a manner as to produce an analysis in the interest of those about whom knowledge is being constructed. It is that frame for the research that establishes the orientation of the analysis and redresses the exclusion of some knowers. This is quite a different matter from democratizing the interpersonal relations among the researchers and informants. The research design does not address or control the direct interpersonal relations among those involved – feminists and disability researchers have written extensively about this. Attention to both issues is important and necessary and, as Campbell et al. suggest, maintaining good working relationships in research is serious and demanding work. Among other things, it calls for high levels of commitment to the shared goals of the research and discriminating skills in interpersonal communication. But even the best personal interaction among the researchers and the subjects of research cannot compensate for an inadequate conceptualization of power in the research.

Data Collection: How to "Look" and "Listen"

We have already established that understanding the social ontology of institutional ethnography is important to data collection. By social ontology we mean that institutional ethnographers understand everyday life to be *constituted by people* whose activities are coordinated in specific ways. For that reason, we must collect data that captures detailed accounts of those activities.

When institutional ethnographers conduct observations, besides making note of what is happening, they listen for the sort of informants' talk that contains and expresses their expertise of living their lives. That way of talking – expressing one's expertise of how to be a competent participant of a setting – can be contrasted with commonsense theorizing about one's life. The latter is also a common way of talking, particularly in answer to questions about why a person does certain things. If researchers ask them, informants will give their views and opinions, and sometimes that is what researchers want to hear. For instance, much research knowledge is generated from surveying people's perceptions and attitudes. In a survey, the researcher would have already determined what set of indicators in people's answers she would be able to code as referencing "the research topic." From those data, framed by adequate theory, the researcher is able to arrive at meanings. Ethnographers who interview or observe informants may also look for themes and then code recurrent topics or words. Whether quantitative or qualitative analysis is done, these kinds of research activities are constructing objectively the phenomenon in discourse. To do so, institutional ethnographers believe, is to lose its meaning as situated activity. Recurring events or recurring use of words have a different interest for institutional ethnographers who are looking for how things happen *here*, in the same way they happen *over there*. Recursivity in institutional ethnography shows a pattern in the world – something is organized to recur, and that is the organization that institutional ethnographers explore.

Here again is where the social ontology of institutional ethnography offers its researchers the basis for an alternative way of knowing about the world. We want to study things that are being lived, experienced and, concurrently or subsequently, talked about. We want to understand how they happen *that particular way.* We find and use data to discover material connections between what actually happens to participants in a research setting and what triggers those particular actions or events. This requires data that differs from data used in research that codes indicators in people's talk into themes, topics, or variables. Data collection for institutional ethnography requires researchers to know the difference between the two kinds of analysis. They must then work out how to have informants talk to them in ways that offer the data they can use for this purpose.

A related hazard for data collectors in institutional ethnography is the way that people talk in professional language about their work. As any outsider who has listened in on a conversation between two co-workers knows, insider language may make it impossible for the outsider to understand what is happening. The people who work in a large organization, for instance, will be members of a discourse that has a shared language, beliefs and values, ways of working, and so on. Ellen Pence (2001) writes about seeing this take place in the criminal justice system where she was conducting research. Moreover, she draws attention to how the shared language and protocols construct unassailable ways of knowing clients. She writes that "Members ... are trained to read and write in institutionally recognizable ways. The reader is linked to the writer of a document in such a system not only through the text but through the legal discourse which organizes their professional training. Professionals are trained to translate what they see and hear and gather from the everyday world into professional discourses about that world" (Pence, forthcoming).

In this notion of professional discourse, not only does it contribute a language and authorized practices for conducting the work of an institution, it provides a framing of the way work is thought about and undertaken. Pence puts it this way:

> Workers' tasks are shaped by certain prevailing features of the system, features so common to workers that they begin to see them as natural, as the way things are done and – in some odd way – as the only way that they could be done, rather than as planned procedures and rules developed by individuals ensuring certain ideological ways of interpreting and acting on a case (Pence, forthcoming).

Here Pence identifies a crucial issue for data collection in institutional ethnographies. For members of organizations trained in institutional and professional discourses, talking about their jobs will be done through the template of those discourses. For many such workers, it is almost impossible to have a conversation about work in any other way. Particularly for informants in positions of authority in organizations, or practitioners such as police officers or medical doctors whose work carries strong authority, describing their work may mean insisting that listeners understand things their way (which they see as the only correct way). Being instructed in the official version creates a problem for researchers who are attempting to discover how things work. Sometimes informants submerge what they actually do by glossing it over, speaking of it in terms given in policy or in rules. Pence calls such accounts "ideological." By this she means that the speaker is speaking from a level of how things should be done, how they are arranged to be done, and what is aimed at in organizational practices. The talk references the discourse, not what is or was actually done. Getting an ideological account will be almost useless for institutional ethnography because it misses the underlying level of activity – what actually happens. Most professionals become proficient at speaking about their work, workplaces, clients, and even their own lives in ideological language. Doing so identifies them as a bona fide member of an insider group. In most cases this appreciation and use of a correct orientation is not only a stylistic feature, but it is essential to being a competent practitioner of the work. Of course, what we are identifying as a professional discourse is not exclusive to "the professions" and how professional work is organized. Any form of training and socialization inculcates its own kind of talk and thinking. People in various fields learn insider discourses to demonstrate their belonging and competence. (Think of what you may know about tree planters, hockey players, teens, computer users, or other identifiable groups.)

Field Methods in Institutional Ethnography

The techniques employed in doing interviews and observations in institutional ethnography are the practices of field methods that any ethnographer would use. Perhaps the key point about using field methods in institutional ethnography is figuring out what, out of all the possibilities, is useful to observe or otherwise pay attention to and record. For this reason, this chapter on data collection is focused, not on field techniques per se, but on the way that data will be used in analysis. We want to answer the question "in institutional ethnography, what are useful data?"

Personal accounts can be a rich resource for institutional ethnography if researchers can learn how to see, hear about, and otherwise understand what people *do* in the course of their everyday lives. This is the content of what Smith calls the "generous concept of work" when she discusses its importance to data collection in institutional ethnography. By the generous concept of work Smith means that everything that people know how to do and that their daily lives require them to do is a data resource. Accounts of this kind can be data whether or not people recognize as work what they are doing in the course of doing their lives. Using Smith's "generous concept of work" allowed Fran Gregor (1994, 2001) to recognize as nurses' work many kinds of activities that hospital nurses carry out to make patients and doctors act in ways that coincide with routines set up for organizational reasons. Her nurse participants had understood what they were doing as "being helpful" or doing what they had to do to get the job done, but never as "nursing." Yet these activities occupied much of their time and required the application of their knowledge and judgement. They were certainly necessary for the hospital's effective administration. Such a constricted view of nursing work prevents nurses from seeing how they are implicated in ruling relations. Using the generous concept of work brings the everyday world of nursing into focus, instead of confining the researcher to the same discursive plane as, for instance, Gregor's nurse subjects. What subjects are actually doing, regardless of how they understand and name their work within professional and organizational discourse, then becomes data for analysis.

Professional language simply obscures what people actually do. For instance when someone says, "I processed that application," or "I manage the household finances," the actualities of the work are missing. The alternative would be to describe how the person did it, using a narrative account that lists the steps, the time used, and so on. The generous account would illustrate the knowledge, skills, and experiences involved. It would name the participants, and the account would show the difficulties to be overcome as well as the tensions absorbed as part of doing the work. If an account were made of managing the household finances as *work*, it could no longer remain an abstract undertaking, with no subject, no particular object of action, and no social relations.

About Observations

Once you, the researcher, know that people's work of conducting their everyday lives is what you are looking for, your ability to interview and observe will be more effective. Going into the field to conduct observations is always an open-ended undertaking, because clearly the observer must be open to see what is happening. Yet within that range of possibilities, only some kinds of observations are relevant to the institutional ethnographic analysis. Let's look at the following instance and see how these observations are relevant.

Marie Campbell observed home support agency staff assigning work to service providers. As she entered the field (in this case, a home support agency) she had in her mind an implicit conceptual frame for her observations. It originated from having developed with her research team a problematic for inquiry about health care provision in general and about the provision of home support services to people with disabilities, in particular. Having already mapped the sequence of institutional events that constituted provision of home support services to clients, she knew that the work she would be seeing would be someone assigning hours of contract work to home support workers. She had no idea about how these assignments were done, except that an agency scheduler used a computer and a telephone and operated out of a room in a particular building. When she arrived, Marie met the supervisor who was her agency contact, and was taken to the scheduling room and introduced to the scheduler, Sandy. They chatted for a few minutes, with Marie explaining her interest in seeing what the work of scheduling was and how the scheduler did her job. Sandy signed a consent form and Marie was given permission to turn her tape on from time to time while she was there. When Sandy said that the computer did the work, Marie asked to sit close enough to the computer screen to watch while Sandy operated it. Marie had a notepad and a pen. Soon the telephone rang and Marie listened to Sandy's side of the conversation When the conversation finished, Sandy explained the situation and what she was going to do. Over the course of the next two hours, this kind of interaction continued. Telephone calls came in and Sandy made calls. She accessed computer screens and consulted them to find available and appropriate workers. She made assignments by modifying data in the system, calling workers, and so on. Sandy talked about her available options, the nature of the problems that arose and how she worked with them. Sometimes Marie asked questions and taped the exchange; sometimes she just listened, watched and wrote notes. She came away with six pages of notes and a double-sided audiotape recording.

The audiotape was transcribed into a text consisting of twenty-five pages. The first exchange that was recorded began like this:

Marie: *Let me get you to say that again. You've taken a ...?*

Sandy: *I've taken an order from the hospital. A lady's being discharged. I have to set her up for this evening, increase her service. I have to notify all the workers to restart and make sure that I do a dated note on the computer and send it to the appropriate field supervisor so that they know that she's home.*

Marie: *So "restart" means she was in ...*

Sandy: *She was on service before. Then she went into hospital and she's coming home now. She's waiting placement. It's going to take about four months for her to get into placement.*

Marie: *A Long Term Care Facility?*

Sandy: *Yeah. Right now she is not really well enough to be at home, but she is not really sick enough to be in the hospital. So it's kind of a waiting game. Hopefully she can manage at home with what we're doing. She's at Willingham, which is independent living.*

Marie: *Willingham?*

Sandy: *It's independent living. They will not keep people there that need any extensive amounts of care. So she has to be placed as soon as possible, but they are saying four months is pretty much the standard wait.*

Marie: *"They" is ...?*

Sandy: *It's Mary Moffitt, the hospital liaison.*

Marie: *How does she get involved?*

Sandy: *The woman was admitted to hospital, from Willingham, now she is being discharged back there with her regular hours plus an increase in service.*

Marie: *You mean that she has home support in an independent living facility?*

Sandy: *We have other people getting service in that building, as well. It has to be on a short-term basis.*

A break in the transcription occurs, then it continues:

Marie: *So we were talking about the "dated note." I'm trying to figure out the difference between dated notes and notes to workers. You were telling me that there's a couple of screens for dated notes, but all of them are for office use and to keep track of the client forever. It's like a chart.*

Sandy: *Yes, exactly.*

Marie: *So you were going to tell me something about them?*

Sandy: *Well, everything that goes into that client's chart is sent to the appropriate field supervisor in the form of a message. And the field supervisor will go through these dated notes. If they find anything specifically interesting about a client – like they are cancelling all the time, or that they fell two weeks ago. She'll watch that client.* (From the interview transcript)

We can look at this excerpt and review what is going on, to try to see what Marie is making of this as "observations." As the observation begins, a telephone call comes in to the scheduler that initiates her response. The scheduler tells Marie about it, but in "professional language" that Marie cannot fully grasp. She asks to have it repeated. This first comment from the scheduler is packed with information about the work and the community health care system and how the scheduler is part of it. For example, there is the issue of "the order" from the hospital, which we later hear was from the hospital-community liaison nurse, whom Sandy treats as a familiar voice on the phone, a participant in her own work process. With a query about whom Sandy is calling "they," Marie is able to turn, in her mind, to a conceptual "map" of how referrals are done. She can place Mary Moffitt in her organizational role and recognize that there is a set of rules about home support that are in play here. The discharged woman is to be "set up for the evening," whatever that means. Marie picks up on the term "re-start" and questions it. Later, we see that she also comes back to the "dated note" for an explanation of what it is and what it accomplishes.

As "data," any of these words and other insider language from the above excerpt might be treated as a clue to the next steps in the inquiry. They might have suggested who else knew important things about the process and who, therefore, might be interviewed. The relevance of any of these pieces of data is how they help the researcher explicate the issues of "provision of home support services." As it happens, the scheduler continued throughout the two hours of observations to come back and work on the problem of finding someone available and appropriate to pick up the "increase in service" to this particular woman. She had trouble finding staff to assign to the "restarted" and expanded care. Sandy's explanation about her work included her knowledge of her options about assigning hours to workers, how she drew from the information before her on the screen, or what she knew from her experience of working with the home support staff who held regular assignments in that Independent Living facility. She talked about why it was important to assign the work to someone who already knew the client. As she worked through screen after screen, she shared her thinking about the difficulties she was facing. As she made her choices amongst the staff available to take the extra assignment, she kept finding reasons why a particular worker was not appropriate. Besides thinking about who already knew the client, a potential worker might be passed over because of her employment status (regular or part-time) and its implications for available working hours. Or her seniority might determine whether or not she could be assigned. For example, perhaps giving her more hours would put a worker into "overtime" and that, Sandy said, needed to be avoided. Information about these organizational issues was programmed into the computer for the scheduler's use.

All this had relevance to the explication of "continuity of care" in this study. Consistency of workers had been identified as a real need for people with disabilities and as something that home support agencies also considered an important part of their service. The data collected were relevant because they offered insights into how continuity of care was compromised through routine features of the organization. Of course, along with this story, elements of other stories were collected that might have been used to explicate other questions about provision of services. When observations and data collection are happening, the researcher will not know exactly how the analysis will make use of the various pieces of data, but she will recognize the relevance to the inquiry. The researcher carries a sense of the research problematic into every observational site and will see elements of what is happening that appear to touch on it. Data are useful to the extent that the stories collected are detailed, explicit, and understandable – as we can see beginning to happen here in the transcribed observations (plus Marie's handwritten notes) of what the scheduler was doing and why she was doing it.

Other lively examples of the use of observations in institutional ethnography appear in Gerald DeMontigny's analysis of his own professional behaviour as a child protection worker (Campbell and Manicom 1995, 209-20). Tim Diamond's (1992) observations of his work as a nursing assistant include reported conversation with patients and with other staff, some of whom offered advice and instruction about the work. The observational work conducted by these two institutional ethnographers differs from Marie Campbell's (above) in that these researchers are recording and reflecting on their own work practices which were already very well known to them. If you need to get to know a setting that is new to you, you may want to conduct significant amounts of observational work. In that case, be prepared to have piles of transcripts that you will not use in your analysis. It is typically the case that very little, but very specific, data is needed for an analysis in institutional ethnography.

About Interviews

Institutional ethnographers use interviews at any stage of an inquiry. Marjorie DeVault and Liza McCoy (2002), in their definitive work on interviewing in institutional ethnography, suggest that interviewing might better be called "talking to people" (756) because it stretches across a continuum from appointments scheduled specifically for the purpose, all the way to serendipitous opportunities that arise when one is going about one's daily life. Yet whether on formal or informal occasions, whether the talking is one-on-one or in a group, the purpose of interviews in institutional ethnography is to "investigate widespread and discursive processes" (DeVault and McCoy 2002, 757). They also insist that "given that the purpose of the interviewing is to build up an understanding of the coordination of activity in multiple sites, the interviews need not be standardized"(757). Interviewees will be chosen as the research progresses, and as the researcher learns more and more about the topic. She will see what she needs to know and will find out who would know it.

DeVault and McCoy's definition of interviewing would also apply to the example of talk (above) occurring during an observation. That excerpt illustrates how, in an interview, it may help to focus on a particular incident that interests you and zero in on what the informant knows about it. You might ask the person to tell you *how* they do what they do. If not conducted during an observation, it may help to suggest that the informant try to remember when they last did what they want to describe. Tell the person to recall that particular incident, where they were, and explain what happened, first, next, etc. without omitting anything. The aim is to get a clear account of how things go together to make up what the informant might consider standard practice without his omitting anything he takes for granted. You may need to check your understanding from time to time, saying "am I getting this right?" and "so then you did so and so, is that right?," or, "what am I missing here?" The test of whether or not you are getting a professional account as opposed to an account of what actually happened, is if you, the listener, cannot see every step without having to imagine pieces. You must be attentive and avoid the ordinary conversational etiquette where people assist each other in making meaning. It is tempting to plug in the missing pieces from one's own knowledge. Or we nod, when someone says, "you know" instead of completing the sentence. As interviewers, we must resist doing that. It may be especially difficult for researchers who share the informant's professional discourse to avoid assisting when a sketchy and discourse-filled account is being given. As an insider to a particular sort of talk, you may not even hear that something has been missed. In polite conversation, we all become competent at making sense in the accepted ways. Interviewers may feel silly asking what seem like obvious questions to clarify things that ordinarily they could be counted on to just know. Questions need to be asked at every point in the story where the steps are skipped or discourse words substitute for "what actually happens."

This is the point where institutional ethnography's roots in ethnomethodology show. Dorothy Smith says "At every point we attempt to view our topic or subject matter, the object of our inquiry, as practices, methods, procedures – as activity, rather than as an entity." This harks back to the ancient ethnomethodological interest in accomplishment and practice (Smith 1990b, 90). Ethnomethodologists saw that members' methods express a certain kind of competence and knowledge that they apply skillfully and in commonsensical ways. A classic example of members' competence is that of queuing at a bus stop or lining up to pay for one's groceries. An ethnomethodologist understands a queue by seeing people doing it (in contrast to trying to define it). The knowledge and skills that one brings to queuing come from ordinary daily practice in conducting one's life as a public transit rider or grocery shopper. As people do this sort of ordinary thing, they bring into being or accomplish the particular features of their lives that the researcher could be studying. They bring those features, such as a queue, into being for researchers to see. This is (what we mean by) social ontology. And that is why, in order to collect data that can be used to understand people's lives, we have to use methods that capture accounts of people actually doing things.

Yet knowing accurately and being able to make claims about what is going on does not emerge from a straightforward reporting of people's work, either first hand or reported accounts. Institutional ethnography aims at more than description of people's knowledge and experiences. People's knowledge and actions are already organized before they talk about them, and they get worked up as they are talked about. Both those who live them and those who research them play parts in this working up. Institutional ethnographers believe that as people bring into being whatever happens, what they do and what they understand and can tell about are shaped through organized processes. (An example: Sandy told Marie that it was important to assign staff who already knew the clients. She believed that she was being attentive to this organizational value but her choices of who to schedule into particular jobs were constrained by other organizational priorities. If she noticed the result, she rationalized it as a necessary compromise. It did not shake her faith, nor that of her agency, that they practised "client-centred" home support. That policy held sway in spite of the routine organizational practices that undermined it.)

Institutional ethnographers inquire into how things like that actually happen. The data they collect is used to discover and illuminate linkages within and across boundaries of settings. Talk about the work undertaken in a setting offers clues to how social relations that operate across its boundaries organize it. Dorothy Smith contends that when anyone speaks in a sensible and coherent manner about their lives, they also speak its social relations. Interviews are one method of capturing informants' talk in ways that direct analysis towards the social relations of the setting. Embedded in informants' talk about their work, generously defined, is their tacit knowledge of how to do it, how to concert their own pieces of the work with the work of others and how to work with the texts that coordinate action. All these activities contribute to what we mean by social relations. We have seen (in the case of the home support scheduler, above) how texts may be at the centre of people's routine enactment of everyday life – of what their own thinking and action can come to. Both interviews and observations of people at work may generate data that identify or offer clues as to their use of texts – with the outcome of crossing experiential boundaries and carrying definite meanings into other sites.

About Texts as Data

Texts appear in people's talk because they are an integral part of what people do and know. The texts that researchers see being used by informants during field observations are often central to everything that happens. Therefore to understand the setting and to explicate the problematic arising in it, texts are a very useful ethnographic data source. Their analytic use will vary, depending upon the nature of the inquiry being conducted. Sometimes publicly available brochures or forms will suggest some avenue to follow to help fill in what the researcher needs to know. Perhaps a text will reference an office, a program, or a policy. More frequently in institutional ethnography, rather than being used as sources of factual information, texts are relied on as crystallized social relations. Institutional ethnographers consult them as an alternative to, and an antidote for, accepting ideological accounts. In Marie Campbell's observations of the home support agency scheduling, the text at the centre of the work was a computer screen. In the research being conducted, there were contrasting stories and beliefs about the provision of home support. In interviews with people with disabilities, clients had complained, sometimes bitterly, about lack of continuity of care workers. They might have one of any number of workers coming into their homes to bathe, dress, or otherwise help them manage their daily lives. This was the source of much dissatisfaction. Graphic accounts were given (and appeared to ethnographic observers) about the problems this created. Conversely, the regional community health authorities and the home support agencies contracted to do home support work had quite another story to tell. The official documents, and the workers themselves, claimed that they offered client-centred services. The computer software was counted on to make scheduling and follow-up effectively and efficiently client-centred.

The researcher was shown how the scheduler was using the computer program, how the different screens held different kinds of information and how those screens guided the scheduler's process of "scheduling." As she watched and listened, Marie saw how scheduling work integrated various organizational priorities into the scheduler's decision making but that was consciously directed towards reducing the number of people going into people's homes. The resulting analysis showed the work process organized in relation to a text in which the organizational priorities (held in computer files) came to subordinate a client-based focus. Understanding the way that the text organized decisions was crucial to this piece of analysis. It superseded the scheduler's interest in continuity of care. In this case, the knowledge claim that could be made was that the agency's intentions to be client-centred was just that, good intentions. What actually happened was quite different.

Texts come into a researcher's hands in many different ways. Many are publicly available. Janet Rankin (2000) analyzed the text of a patient satisfaction survey circulated to a member of her own family who had been a patient in a British Columbia hospital. It became an important piece of evidence for use in Rankin's doctoral research on the restructuring of nursing work in contemporary hospitals. The patient satisfaction survey helped her explicate the puzzle she discovered around different views and beliefs regarding hospital nursing in settings that are being restructured by increasingly sophisticated forms of information-based decision making. Hospital authorities tend to argue that nursing is not being targeted for change and hospital re-structuring is not altering it. Rankin's nurse informants know differently and her research goal was to find and make the concrete links (through explication). A variety of hospital management and nursing texts, including the patient satisfaction survey, helped Rankin to build an argument showing the material connections between new modes of hospital and health care organization and both the planned and unplanned alterations in how nurses conduct their work.

Whether or not the institutional ethnographer's data come from field research, interviews or texts, the research will not be done until she exposes the linkages between different kinds or levels of data. To be able to move from local accounts and local action to the social relations of ruling, research must be conducted at different levels. What we have called entry points are places where the problematic of interest is going on and people can talk about it through their involvement in it. Entry to the social relations organizing the setting is facilitated by careful attention to data at that level. Entry-level research must be complemented by the collection of data at sites beyond local experiences, outside the boundaries of what informants at the local level know. The data sought outside or beyond people's experiential accounts, we have called second-level data. It is the analytic use of both levels of data that distinguishes institutional ethnography from its ethnographic cousins. The data-collection process in institutional ethnography calls for a process of tracking back or following clues forward from the local site and the data collected there. This aspect of data collection also requires analytic thinking, explained in Chapter Five. Data collection cannot be done at the second level without conceptualizing the connections between the two. Theory is therefore an essential background component of data collection. Bringing data together with theory happens explicitly in the process of analysis.

Chapter Five

Analyzing Data in Institutional Ethnography

Once you have collected your data, you are confronted with the problem of what to do with it. Some sense *must* be made of it. Although making sense is the purpose behind conducting any research, the particular aims of institutional ethnography direct the kind of sense that is to be made. Also, the task of presenting the research findings coherently and persuasively, perhaps as a thesis or as a research report or article, is part of doing this kind of analysis. In writing the analysis, your goal is to make the research product not only understandable but also convincing. Analysis means deciding what you are going to be able to say on the basis of the data you have collected. But a convincing presentation of your research also relies on having or gaining the necessary writing skills, including how to make an argument. Like any qualitative research writing, the fundamentals of essay writing are important to making your account persuasive.

By this stage, the story to be told from your data has already begun to make itself apparent – that is, if you have followed the approach to data collection suggested here. This whole book has been a preparation for your discovery of the workings of social relations in everyday life that you have wanted to explore. This notion is part of the conceptual framework that has guided your search for data and your subsequent analysis. You have collected data on people conducting their lives, and have begun to understand that their everyday activities are somehow being coordinated. Now you must begin to make those connections and their implications explicit for others to understand. This next step is analysis. Your task is to enable others to see what you see, so writing is an integral part of your analytic work. As you begin to write, you must maintain your interest in what is actually happening in the settings you have been examining. Explication of that actuality is the analytic practice that institutional ethnographers must learn, and some of the ins and outs of that learning appear next.

Moving From Data to Data Analysis: What Path to Follow?

Many researchers find the data-collection phase of ethnography exciting but dread the prospect of doing the analysis. It is likely to seem a particularly mysterious undertaking for those who are new to institutional ethnography. Even if they understand the major ideas of institutional ethnography, students may find themselves almost completely at a loss about how to proceed from the data towards the finished research account or product. That does not mean they have learned nothing from collecting their data. Even beginning researchers find themselves learning things about the setting and the situations they are researching, as they conduct interviews or make observations. Of course, seeing connections may not reduce their anxiety about doing analysis. Their very success at recognizing how intertwined their problematic is with all sorts of other issues, people, and places may be upsetting. It can create a feeling of being overwhelmed by the enormity of what they are studying. Rather than clarifying what their study can show, learning about the complexity of their topics may be depressing. They may doubt their capacity to focus on a discrete piece of what they are learning. They may begin to question how they are ever going to be able to make sense of it, and not least produce an account of it that others will understand. Methods texts that offer advice and instructions about ethnography all seem to agree that focusing, choosing the right question, matching up the data and the question one asks, are all crucial to successful analysis. But, for this phase as for others, the methods texts are silent about differences in analyzing data in institutional ethnography as compared to other ethnographies.

Finding no clear instructions for this phase of institutional ethnography poses a challenge. Confronted with mounds of data, you may wonder how to tell what is most important to write about? If it is all equally important, where does one begin? This is a critical moment at which many wrong turnings can be taken, out of confusion and anxiety to be doing something. There is always description to fall back on. You may begin to write up everything you did and everything you were told. Or, realizing that this is an impossible task, you may turn to coding your data, to discover themes. When one is searching for a way to reduce confusion, identifying the replication of themes across informants may seem relevant or at least rational. Counting instances of comparable events, themes, or language usage may seem useful. You ask yourself "wouldn't it be significant if more than one person talked about the same thing, for instance?" Computer programs designed to help manage qualitative data by categorizing them may only add to the institutional ethnographer's troubles rather than helping (but see DeVault and McCoy 2002, 768-9). The main analytic notion to hold on to, at this point, is the idea of social relations at the heart of your research interest. You do not want to categorize your data in ways that are artificial, or that distort and obscure the relations at the crux of the institutional ethnography. The meaning of the data is in their setting of use as they arise there. That is why suggestions to cut up and sort one's data are likewise unhelpful, if not downright dangerous. Such strategies contain vestiges of methodologies and epistemologies foreign to institutional ethnography. But if this is the *wrong* way to go about analysis, what is the *right* way?

A guiding query to use as you read your collection of data analytically is "what does it tell me about how this setting or event happens as it does?" Many experienced institutional ethnographers would agree with Eric Mykhalovskiy when he points out that "analytic thinking begins in the (data-collection) interview"(DeVault and McCoy 2002, 757). His comment arises in the context of explaining to DeVault and McCoy how he conducts interviews with informants. Mykhalovskiy suggests that in "talking to people" he is "checking his understanding as it develops" (757) in contrast to going to an interview with a prepared set of questions to be asked and answered. In a conversational way he can offer up his developing understanding to the informant for confirmation or correction. He is reminding us that, as with other ethnographies, institutional ethnographers want to understand their informants and be absolutely clear about what is being said, meant, etc. Informants are experts in doing what they routinely know how to do. Each informant's story helps the researcher see more of the emerging big picture but there is more to analysis than producing accounts that informants can recognize. A successful analysis supersedes any one account and even supersedes the totality of what informants know and can tell. Ellen Pence is alluding to this in the manual describing the Safety and Accountability Audit of domestic violence intervention that she has designed (Pence and Lizdas 1998). In the following excerpt, she identifies additional sources of information on how an informant's experience gets structured outside of her own knowing about it.

Experiential methods (and accounts of experience) can only go so far in drawing an accurate map of how a victim's lived experience becomes interpreted into the system designed to protect her and hold her abuser accountable. To complete the picture, auditors also need to look at how the paper trail created by each agency serves these goals (Pence and Lizdas 1998, 33).

Pence points to aspects of how agencies structure "what goes on," what happens to people. This, too, is data that add to what people know and can tell about their lives. Institutional ethnographers are attempting to *explicate* everyday experiences and people's accounts of them, not just collect and describe them. The explication of experiences calls for yet another level of researching, data collection, and analysis, and is a distinctive feature of institutional ethnography. Because characteristic difficulties arise for newcomers to institutional ethnography at this point in analysis, we have inserted a section here to try to address them. Explication of ethnographic data, as institutional ethnographers do it, takes their analysis in a different direction from identifying themes or theorizing data. In the following section, we discuss how analytic strategies differ across different ethnographic approaches. We hope that this little excursion into *other ways* of analyzing ethnographic data may help new institutional ethnographers clarify how their own analysis proceeds and why institutional ethnography is done the way it is.

Different Ethnographies, Different Analytic Strategies

Analytic strategies, however tentative or prescriptive, vary considerably across the different traditions within ethnography. Similarities across ethnographic traditions seem self-evident – one goes into the field and listens, observes, and gathers whatever information helps in understanding what people are doing. Differences arise in ethnography, as in other scholarship, when researchers attend differently to what observations mean. Different ontologies (beliefs about the nature of social reality) require the use of different analytic strategies. The social ontology of institutional ethnography discussed in earlier chapters underpins everything that one does as method, including how data are worked with.

Analysis, as we said earlier, is about making some particular meaning from the data. Making meaning in a manner that stands up to the relevant tests is the purpose of any scholarly analysis. Researchers must establish the validity, warrantability, or truth-value of their analysis within the tenets of its particular methodology. Findings are evaluated by asking, "Did the researcher demonstrate that she used the procedures that are relevant to her declared methodology in arriving at these analytic conclusions?" A quick survey of various instructions and explanations available for conducting analysis shows that ethnographers subscribe to a wide range of world-views and epistemologies, at least implicitly. Analytic procedures appropriate to one situation may not be appropriate to another. Hammersley and Atkinson (1995) review beliefs about the nature of reality that underlie different ethnographies, and help to match up analytic processes to belief systems. They also give a sense of how shifts in thinking about the sociology and philosophy of knowledge cumulatively alter qualitative and ethnographic research. For instance, much of the difference found in ana-lytic methods can be traced to how the researcher understands, or ignores, her own contribution to the account being generated. Beliefs about how to know the field – the researcher's ontological commitments – determine a researcher's view of acceptable approaches to data analysis. Institutional ethnography is grounded in a particular understanding of the relation between the knower and the known. To attempt to clarify the institutional ethnography position on this, we are going to compare it with the stance (and matching analytic strategies) of some other kinds of ethnography.

What some writers refer to as conventional ethnography is the anthropologi-cal version (although, as Whittaker (1994) argues, the anthropological version is not a unitary or static entity). David Fetterman, author of the prestigious *Ethnog-raphy: Step by Step* (1989) is a practitioner of the conventional approach. Fetterman sees the anthropologist as ethnographer: "The ethnographer is interested in understanding a social and cultural scene from the emic, or insider's, perspective. The ethnographer is both storyteller and scientist; *the closer the readers of an ethnog-raphy come to understanding the native's point of view the better the story and the better the science*" (Fetterman 1989, 12, emphasis added).

Fetterman clearly sees the ethnographer's task as the discovery and recording of what informants know about their world. Ethnography, as begun by anthro-pologists, was of primitive cultures. Ethnography was then, and according to Fetterman still is, primarily descriptive in nature (Fetterman 1998, 139, n. 3). He says: "A typical ethnography describes the history of the group, the geography of the location, kinship patterns, symbols, politics, economic systems, educa-tional and socialization systems and the degree of contact between the target culture and the mainstream culture" (22).

Anthropological ethnographers "go and look" and attempt to bring back accounts of "how it is," as objectively as possible. They may think of what they do as understanding the field in its own terms, but Fetterman's account of ethnography as description alerts readers to how description is not simply a technical matter. As the above quotation illustrates, the elements and terms of an anthropological description are pre-theorized. Fetterman's own instructions introduce the novice ethnographer to the anthropological concepts that he says "guide ethnographers in their fieldwork" (Fetterman 1998, 26): for example, culture, symbol, ritual, holistic orientation, perspectives. He expects these concepts to become "automatic" to their work (26). These instructions show the ethnographer to be a certain kind of knower doing a special kind of seeing, hearing and knowing. For Fetterman, the ethnography is fallible, meaning that the anthropologist can get it wrong unless appropriate procedures are used.

Because practitioners of the conventional version of ethnography must exercise skepticism about the accuracy of data they collect, they use analytic strategies for testing the accuracy of *what informants say*. Triangulation is the most common strategy used for this purpose (Denzin 1978; Thomas 1993). Fetterman (1989) also proclaims triangulation to be a basic analytic procedure in (conventional) ethnographic research. In triangulation, data collected from different sources are compared to "test the quality of the information to understand more completely the part an actor plays in the social drama, and ultimately to put the whole situation into perspective" (Fetterman 1998, 89). A researcher working in this mode compiles "what informants said" to generate hypotheses and then tests them against each other to come up with an accurate, or best possible, account of the situation.

A related analytic use of ethnographic data is to theorize about the setting. Grounded theory (Glazer and Strauss 1967) offers analytical techniques that many researchers find useful in selecting and substantiating ideas about what the researcher saw or heard. In grounded theory, analysis aims for abstraction, not just description. Schreiber (2001) says that grounded theorists try to construct meanings that account for how participants understand their lives and solve the problems occurring in them. A complex set of analytic procedures is followed to produce the concepts, categories, and eventually the "theory," that explains participants' experiences, *as they understand them.*

Grounded theory's interest in analysis that explores and explains informants' perspectives is shared with symbolic interactionists. In an article explaining ethnographic inquiry in the symbolic interactionist tradition, Prus explains that:

(symbolic interactionism) is an examination of the ways that people make sense of their situations and work out their activities in conjunction with others. Human experience is not to be dismissed as subjective, epiphenomenal, or non-factual. Since people know the world only as they experience it, and people experience the world in an intersubjective manner, then this realm of inquiry (human experiences within a world of others) becomes the paramount reality to which researchers should attend in their investigations of human group life. (Prus 1994, 20-1)

Prus suggests that the ontology of symbolic interactionism is social. People are understood to put their lives together interactionally and symbolically and this view underpins the analytic procedures used. Important topics for research attention thus arrive from informants' viewpoints, interpretations of themselves and others, their attempts to influence others, their relationships and the history of their encounters and exchanges. Ethnographers working in this tradition look for how people "do" everyday life rather than for (external) causes and effects. The central research interest is to capture and display the strategies people themselves employ moment-to-moment, denoting "a realm of human agency and enterprise rooted in an awareness of the intersubjective other" (Prus 1994, 26).

As in grounded theory, analysis of data aims at how the individual experience can be generalized. Symbolic interactionists use theoretical concepts (Prus calls them "generic" concepts) to transcend single instances of ethnography. The use of generic concepts draws single instances, descriptions of individual cases, etc., into theory to "make something" *generalizable* of the data. This explanatory direction towards abstraction is shared with grounded theory. In contrast, institutional ethnography's interest in explication is materialist and empirical. To "make something" of data in institutional ethnography, researchers go back to the field to discover actual connections. Speaking in theoretical terms about their analytic work, institutional ethnographers would say that they explicate the ruling relations that organize and coordinate the local experiences of informants. Generalizability in institutional ethnography relies on discovery and demonstration of how ruling relations exist in and across many local settings, organizing the experiences informants talked about.

While the institutional ethnographer is interested in collecting data that display insiders' knowledge (thus our interest in informants' descriptions of their "work" discussed in Chapter Four), the ultimate purpose of the institutional ethnography is *not* to produce an account *of* or *from* those insiders' perspectives. Where ethnographers in the conventional mode conduct tests (for example, triangulation) to give evidential weight to specific views, the institutional ethnographer attempts to explicate how the local settings, including local understandings and explanations, are brought into being – so that informants can talk about their experiences as they do. Institutional ethnographers, like ethnographers who use symbolic interactionist theory, understand an ethnographic setting to be constituted locally by people's work. However, theorizing that work and those understandings, as grounded theorists and symbolic interactionists do, is not the analytic goal of institutional ethnography. Getting to an account that explicates *the social relations* of the setting is what an institutional ethnographic account is about. This kind of analysis uses what informants know and what they are observed doing for the analytic purpose of identifying, tracing and describing the social relations that extend beyond the boundaries of any one informant's experiences (or even of all informants' experiences). Translocal and discursively-organized relations permeate informants' understandings, talk, and activities. An institutional ethnography must therefore include research into those elements of social organization that connect the local setting and local experiences to sites outside the experiential setting. Analysis in institutional ethnography is directed to explication that builds back into the analytic account what the researcher discovers about the workings of such translocal ruling practices. These are some of the important theoretical and ontological differences that distinguish analysis of data in institutional ethnography.

Making Sense of Discursively-Organized Settings

As many writers explaining ethnographic methods indicate, the world of ethnography is changing. Anthropologists working at the end of the twentieth century recognized that primitive settings were fast disappearing under the pressures of globalization. Societies under study are all being influenced by Western/Northern industrialization. Even a cursory consideration of how North Americans and Europeans live reveals differences in the warp and weft of the contemporary social fabric from earlier times. In Canada, prior to the 1950s, the differences between some aspects of our lives and those of so-called primitive cultures might not have been so distinctive. Not too long ago, for example, many Canadians lived in communities surrounded by their extended families and produced their own food. Now multinational or transnational corporations and mass media "brand" our daily lives. Canadians have become consumers orientated to a global market, even for our food. Reports from the South Pacific atolls suggest that so-called primitive cultures buy some of the same food products as we do and suffer similar (environmentally orientated) perplexity about the disposal of its packaging. Whereas these island people until recently would have had closely interlocking kinship patterns and family life, now their families, like ours, are fragmented by employment across vast distances and by schedules not of their or our own making. The effects of these social organizational changes on local settings are apparent. For instance, in Canada, contemporary employment patterns may require parents to work outside the home. Daycare for children then becomes an issue when members of the extended family, who in previous generations would have assumed responsibility for the care of the child, are now living thousands of miles away. The discourse on childcare may continue to express values arising in earlier times. It may confirm or conflict with parents' views and their everyday experiences.

The point is that social life has crucial "meanings" organized outside local settings where people live and from which they speak when they talk about their experiences. Late-twentieth-century scholars have been exploring and debating the extent to which everything we know about our lives is discursively organized. This feature of social life is currently an important and unifying topic across different disciplines (besides sociology, feminist, and literary studies where it has engaged scholars for several decades). Disciplinary traditions are being rethought by, among others, Moss (2001) in geography, Purkis (forthcoming) in nursing, Scott (1991) in history, Chambon (1999) in social work. Previously authoritative ways of knowing appear to fail or are discredited. It becomes apparent to researchers who accept the implications of a discursively-organized world that the conventional approach to ethnography, "going and looking," falls short as a way of knowing. Or, at least, data collected through traditional ethnographic methods are being subjected to new theories and new analytic strategies.

It is methodologically important, institutional ethnographers insist, to be attentive to how someone, speaking about their life, misses its social organization. In order to discover and disclose how its taken-for-granted social organization is meaningful for what happens, a specialized inquiry must be conducted. For researchers convinced of the importance of the discursive organization of everyday life, the social organization of knowledge is useful theory and institutional ethnography is a relevant analytic approach.

Writing Analysis in Institutional Ethnography

Understanding the theory that informs institutional ethnography is the necessary framework for analysis but it is not a sufficient guide to writing it. Researchers must take some practical steps to make something of their data. There are some openings to be found in the apparently blank wall that confronts the new institutional ethnographer with mounds of ethnographic data and no convenient schema for analytic writing. Institutional ethnographers have developed various practices for proceeding. In this section, some practical suggestions and illustrations are offered to help researchers build on the ideas that emerge as the data is collected.

One recommendation to assist in your movement towards analysis is to find someone with whom you can talk about what you are learning from your data. Begin to try to explain to someone else what you now see. Listen to their questions and try to answer comprehensively. Watch yourself drawing on what your informants have told you, or what you learned in your observations, or from textual materials that you have gathered from the settings you studied. As you talk, make notes to yourself about what chunks of data illuminate the stories you are able to tell. Notice also when you cannot answer a question you are asked. This kind of informal storytelling may help you to decide what elements of your data to include in your analytic writing. It may also suggest how your analysis is going to have boundaries established by the specificity of the data you have collected. Seeing what you can and cannot speak to from your data is real progress.

Notice when you want to say, in answer to a query about your story, "but that is not really relevant to what I am studying." Are you as clear as you might be about what you are studying? Sometimes getting involved in data collection brings up so many interesting issues that you get a bit confused. Here is how your earlier conception of a "problematic" helps. You might want to go back to that writing of the problematic and its conceptual framing to recall what you did and did not understand earlier. Remember that, for developing a focus, you relied on certain experiences that puzzled you and others. You may have had a hunch about the topic that helped you identify a problematic for study. Even though you will have set it aside as you developed your conceptual framework and conducted your fieldwork, that moment of "disjuncture" or "disquiet" motivating your interest in the topic is still analytically important. Now you have dug more deeply and excavated[9] the problematic setting from various angles. Informants speaking from various positions have added their expertise to what you know. You chose them as informants because of some position they occupied that related them to the original setting and your original curiosity. Now you can review your early thoughts informed by all that your informants have told you. There is no technical fix for finding meaning in institutional ethnography. You have to read, think, puzzle, write, and continue in that vein with each element of the data. Your insights will be about how the data illuminate the way that the setting works. You are figuring out the social relations of the setting.

This reflection on the data in conjunction with a review of your problematic offers you a starting point for "writing up the data." Analysis in institutional ethnography is done in your writing and as you write. Your writing begins to make something of your data, to move it towards analysis. It alters your data from an undifferentiated mass – from piles of transcripts, notebooks full of observational notes, boxes of documents – to "analytic writing." Be prepared to write and rewrite. The pieces that you write up now will eventually go together in ways that construct the analysis. Just as you can "tell a story" to a listener, now in writing you are telling a story about what you learned to a reader. You can use "the point" that you saw in your storytelling, to make an analytic point in your writing. Begin there and do not worry about the flow of a chapter at first. Writing a little piece shows you that you have something to say about your data and that you can use them analytically.

Writing up your data into stories begins the process of making use of your data as evidence. Let's say that you want to make a particular analytic point in writing that you have already explained in your storytelling. The idea may seem to have just come to you, but you must search out the evidence for your insight as it occurs in the raw data. You find a piece of raw data, insert it into the text you are writing and then explain what you have already noticed that is relevant (to your problematic) about it. As you do so, you learn what exactly you can say using this piece of data. You need to consider how it supports your developing account. Notice that as you work with it, this piece of data may alter slightly what you thought you were going to say. The data hold your writing to "their" account.

There are some simple but important technical strategies for writing up data into analysis. The goal is to use your data persuasively. Just inserting a blob of data into your writing will not work. As you write, explain to readers the meaning that you have discovered in it, inserting your explanation both before and after the data excerpt that you use. An example of how to write using data as evidence comes from Campbell's (2001) article analyzing the text-mediated assessment of an applicant's needs for community health services. An observer has taped a conversation between a case manager (an employee of the local health care authority) and a man called Tom who has a disability and needs personal care in his home. The case manager doing the assessment is trying to be "client-centred," as is the agency's claim, and is trying to keep Tom fully involved in the decision making about the range of services that might be offered. The argument being made in the article is that, regardless of her intent, the case manager is unable to work in a client-centred way. In the section chosen for use here, Campbell is developing for readers her point that Tom's participation in decision making about community health services is not authentic, that he cannot possibly collaborate equitably in making decisions under the particular circumstances. An excerpt of observational data is used to illustrate what the author sees is actually happening (in contrast to what she will argue later in the paper is an ideologically constructed version of it). The following is an instance of how to support a point an analyst wants to make by using observational data as evidence. The form that the writing takes is important to reading it as analysis. In the first paragraph of the following text, the author makes the point she wants readers to "get," prior to inserting the data:

> All these features of the decision making appear to undermine Tom's sense of being in control of his life and health, regardless of the services the case manager is able to offer. This suggests that caution should be taken in assuming that Tom is really participating authentically in any of these decisions. This becomes even more apparent in the following exchange where the case manager is clearly attempting to include him.

> Case Manager: *Would you like a physio to come and just do maybe a bath assessment and just assess what you're doing and see if there are any aids or little things that could help you with — managing from day to day?*

> Tom: *If it's all right with you, sure, I guess so.*

The author then tells readers what she wants them to "see" in the above exchange. She does not leave them to make their own interpretation. As we read on, we see that she inserts *her* interpretation and that it elaborates the analytic point that she asserted at the beginning of the excerpt. This discussion, that directly follows the data (above), *is analysis of it.*

Notice that the case manager does not say, "I will get the physio to come and see you." She asks Tom's opinion. But Tom's response "if it's all right with you, sure, I guess so," suggests that he may not really understand what is being offered. He is unsure about whether he wants or needs what she is offering. He seems to defer to the case manager's expertise and she does little to correct this imbalance. Without access to adequate information, he cannot make sensible choices. At this point (in the application process) the case manager has information about the health care system, physiotherapy, and other programs and services potentially available to him, none of which he knows about. Client participation requires more than this kind of on-the-spot invitation to agree or disagree. The choice being offered here is definitely not the same thing as Tom having sufficient information to make his participation in decisions viable. Any claim that Tom retains control over his life and the important choices about becoming a client of the agency is not supported by this observed interaction even though we can see that the case manager is attempting to be "client centred". (Campbell, forthcoming)

The goal is to have readers first "hear" your analytic point, then read an excerpt of data that illustrates it. It is not sufficient to throw into the story bits of data that you see as confirming your view. You must explain to readers how "what informants say or do" works as confirmation or evidence. You will want to draw from at least one interview or observation or other data source. You will probably see how to introduce pieces of data from several sources. But remember that, in institutional ethnography, inserting more examples does not necessarily make better analysis.

As you work through your data, you will see that not all stories seem to be pointing in the same direction. You must examine these carefully and account for differences. Do not worry about informants having different experiences and saying different things about them. In institutional ethnography, as discussed earlier in this chapter, informants are not expected to have matching experiences. Analysts discover coherence as they uncover the social relation organizing informants' various experiences and stories about them. You will begin to see how different stories enlarge your overall understanding of what is happening. As you work with your own data, you will continue to clarify your understanding, moving away from your beginning hunch towards an argument that becomes nuanced and useful. In this way, you will find that you are doing analysis.

You are drawing on your data to make one point, as above, which is analytically "interesting." You move on from there to other features showing how the story develops and unfolds.

What you find analytically interesting in your data, if you have followed the process suggested here, will not be irrelevant to your problematic. There are, of course, an almost unlimited number of potential topics that could be explored in any setting and your data could be used in many ways. What is interesting to you will be so precisely because it helps you understand the dynamics of your problematic. Your interest as you go into the field to collect data has already been directed by your preliminary conceptual work. You have developed your research interest by problematizing the situation and the setting of your study. That careful preliminary work focused your attention in a particular way. By becoming engaged in the conceptualization of your study as institutional ethnography, you will have developed your research interest theoretically. You already knew when you collected the data that you were looking to see how the social relations of the setting work, how different actors constitute the setting, etc. As you listened to informants explaining what they do in their everyday life, you already had in your mind the notion of ruling relations, texts operating as extensions of ruling relations, and so on. Now you begin to sort through your data analytically and determine what pieces to use. Reminding yourself of the problematic with which you began helps you identify from your reams of data the pieces that advance your understanding of the problematic.

The following is an example that shows the development of an analytic process from the conceptualization of a problematic to the writing-up of the data and the establishment of an argument – sustainable by the data. As research for her thesis (2001), graduate student Nancy Bell thought that institutional ethnography might help her gain some new insights into a high-profile inquest into the death of a child in British Columbia. The records of the inquest were publicly available for study. Many features of the death and how it was subsequently dealt with were puzzling to Bell, both personally and in her working capacity at the BC Children's Commission. She brought both points of view to the research. To focus on what she would make the problematic for study, Bell had to first examine the relevant data, in this case a number of texts that became part of the exhibits of the inquest or its proceedings. Not until then could she see what her study could address and what puzzles, latent in the setting, might be made visible through close examination of these data.

(A reminder of the practicalities of any research project: certain decisions about the inquiry depend upon what data are going to be accessible.) Owing to the textual nature of Bell's research setting, her inquiry would be confined to textual data.[10] She found herself puzzling as she read through the different texts over differences in how they pictured the child who died. An early expression of her research problematic was "This child became known quite differently to the various people who interacted with her in the last weeks and months of her life." At this early stage in the inquiry Bell wrote that "some accounts took on an authority that led to certain actions or inaction ... and ... they obliterated other accounts"(working notes). That particular action-in-texts was to become the focus of her research, its problematic to be explicated.

The process of inquiry that Bell followed began with her entry to the text-mediated world of inquests and human service work. She undertook her research by exploring the theory of textual action and the analytic use of a "text-reader conversation." Reading the texts analytically would be her method of inquiry into the social relations of such a setting. Institutional ethnography acts as a kind of radiography of everyday life, making visible its skeletal underpinnings. Of course, the skeleton is comprised of people's actions that are coordinated somehow, including textually. Bell, immersing herself in this approach, was simultaneously thinking through how a textual analysis might be done. It was necessary for her to keep in mind that, although she would need to discover who did what with regard to producing and using the texts in question, she had to make her discoveries by following the traces left in those same texts. That was all she had to go on. Her text analysis had to begin with what was in the texts. She had to make sense of them using familiar reading practices.

As she began to write up her data, she saw that the child had come to be known as dying of a terminal illness in the course of the work conducted by health care providers. She recognized that this textual construction was an important element in what actually happened to the child. Bell was then able to be more specific in her formulation of her research problematic as a question about how this knowledge of the child had been produced as authoritative. She identified some specific texts to analyze: a set of records made by health care providers. These texts displayed work processes involving the child and her family. The question of "how the child came to be known as dying of a terminal illness" was a kind of touchstone that Bell could hang on to as she did her reading of the texts and her analytic writing. That was the puzzle to be solved.

The institutional ethnographic character of the textual analysis that Bell conducted made it possible for her to treat the texts as visible traces of certain social relations of the child's life and death. This determined her approach to the analytic reading of the texts. Something had actually happened that occasioned the writing of the health care providers' records. Each worker had activated an organizational text. They each selected features of their work, their observations and decisions about the child, proposed action, etc., for inscription in their records, and, consequently, they de-selected other features. Bell's reading had to make their inscriptions sensible – not in any which way, but as a competent reader of such texts was intended to understand them. Beyond that, her institutional ethnography had to recover and display what the texts accomplished in the child's life and death. Bell's analysis explicated this work of inscription. She discovered how collectively the health care workers' texts constituted the "fact" that the child was "dying of a terminal illness" and how attention to possible neglect of the child was subordinated, and eventually ignored, until the inquest determined her to have died of severe malnutrition.

Interpretation and Analysis

Working with data in institutional ethnography calls for interpretation, or rather, for finding conceptual links in order to make sense of the data. Not just any interpretation will suffice. In institutional ethnography interpretation is disciplined first by the analytic framework of social organization of knowledge and then by the materiality of the data. The connections that are to be made are not theoretical ones – although, as we stress throughout this book, theory guides the problematizing of the research setting, data collection, and analysis. But when it comes to interpreting data, institutional ethnography relies on, explores, and explicates linkages that are lived, brought into existence in time and space by actual people doing actual things. Nancy Bell's argument had to adhere to what she found and could display about what had actually happened in the situation she studied. To do so, she identified and wrote up her argument, bringing in evidence from the texts that constituted both the health care providers' work and the records of that work. She explicated how their ideas, accounts of actions, statements, plans, professional language, etc., appearing in one or more texts recurred, carrying specific meanings across sites of action. She discovered how the idea arose that the child was dying of a terminal illness and then became an officially-accepted view in the texts and was acted on. She found instances of how alternative ideas and potential actions were dropped. She showed that the signing of a Do Not Resuscitate order officially supported palliative care as appropriate intervention, and that it suppressed interest in other potential courses of action.

We are stressing the importance of how an institutional ethnographer writes the analysis that supports her argument. The presentation is frequently a weak point in an otherwise interesting inquiry. Beginning institutional ethnographers are likely to see the linkages that emerge from their inquiry. They usually discover what is happening and are likely to be able to explain it coherently in a verbal presentation. But writing the analysis is more difficult. Sometimes beginning institutional ethnographers begin to assume that readers can see what they see and that they do not really need to describe their basis for knowing. Sometimes their writing lacks sufficient illustrative content to be clear and convincing. The difficulty may be in translating one's developing understanding of how a setting works into an argument that can be substantiated. An argument develops in stages. There is the "seeing" that the institutional ethnographer can do as she reviews her data early on, becoming increasingly explicit as she writes it up into stories. The first statement of argument can be worked up as a kind of sketch of what the data collection allows the researcher to see and understand. That is the basis of a working argument. It helps the researcher select data for ongoing work, including some picking and choosing about which lines of analysis will be followed up and which will not. With the work-up of this early sketch of an argument, the researcher can move on to the next step. Let's say that she has written some stories about discrete pieces of data. She can now collect those pieces and organize them into coherent sections with each addressing a part of the sketched argument. (Sometimes mapping the argument helps – an actual pictorial arrangement of chunks of writing grouped in relation to the argument.) As more pieces of data are analyzed, the original thinking about what was going on can be updated and the argument clarified. The final statement of the argument is what the data allow to be said and what the writing of it actually says.

Analytic interest in institutional ethnography is often in discovering how the conduct of people's lives is coordinated in relation to ruling ideas and practices. From informants' stories and research on how reported events occur, the analyst can figure out what makes things happen as they do. The research will make apparent the people who are involved and how they are involved. Bell's research, for instance, discovered the temporal sequencing of health care intervention. She discovered the emergence in formal and informal health providers' (sequenced) texts of a crystallized view of the child, whom she called Nina. Bell writes what she sees, and what she makes of it:

On May 21, the home care nurse visited [the child's] home after the hospice volunteer telephoned to advise the home care nurse of [the child's] need for service. In the home care nursing records, there is a recording in the "Progress Notes" section [see Appendix D (a)…]

Ten year old girl dying from Rett syndrome apparently was diagnosed [with] disease at 18 months…'

It appears that these notes represent information the home care nurse received from the hospice volunteer prior to the visit to [the child's home] – information that would have guided the home care nurse in her work on the day she conducted [the] assessment. (Bell 2001, 103)

Bell then identifies from the nurses' recording, following the telephone call from the hospice worker, the phrases that articulate with the provincial criteria for admission to palliative care. For instance, she argues that speaking about Rett Syndrome as a disease "fits [this child] within the provincial policy that refers to 'other end-stage diseases'" (Bell 2001, 103). She goes on to compare the nurse's assessment notes to the home care nursing policy for palliative care. She is demonstrating how these workers acted within their proper standards and yet how their choices of observations and language use "worked up" the child, her life, her behaviour, and circumstances to fit the palliative care policy. This is building Bell's evidence for an argument.

Bell's analysis suggests how certain officials such as those of the ministry responsible for child welfare were not brought into the conversation about the child and her family taking place through texts. She explicates the professional and organizational course of action that culminated in a Do Not Resuscitate order. She is getting at an important feature of the social organization of the health providers' work. She shows how the health provider texts were activated, *properly*, in light of organizational and professional rules and expectations. Her explication of textual practices sustains her argument that this textually coordinated work resulted in an account of the child as "dying of a terminal illness," that it authorized subsequent palliative care, and made plausible service providers' inaction around neglect. This example displays what can be learned through institutional ethnography's attention to the coordination or concerting of action that organizes "what happened." Beginning with what is known experientially, talked about, and in this case what appears in textual data, the actual concerting of social relations is discovered and plotted in. Here the policies, professional practices, and organizational interactions, some of which were formal and textually mediated, and some informal and casual, are shown to be ruling what happened. Little by little, from picking at the pieces of data and writing them up, the full argument is made.

Also exemplified in Bell's analysis is the feature of institutional ethnography that makes it most useful to those who want to make changes to practices that oppress or subordinate. At the centre of the analysis is the standpoint of the subject or subjects who occupy the everyday world as the study problematizes it. Bell puts the child at the centre of the analysis. Nina died and Bell answers the question "how did it happen that Nina's life unfolded as it did?" Bell's analysis makes crucial aspects of Nina's life and death visible and understandable; she explicates the institutional processes that account for what happened. The promise of institutional ethnography is that it maintains the subjectivity of those whose experience is problematized. The findings should explicate that experience and reveal what is happening that is relevant *to them*. In focusing on social relations and the institutional processes organizing them, this form of analysis identifies and then illuminates the actual workings of the setting. From an interest in blame, research interest shifts to analysis of processes and practices. How participants are, or were, involved can be made clear. When it is time to put research findings of this sort into practice, they point to the institutional processes that need to be reviewed and changed.

Chapter Six

Putting Institutional
Ethnography into Practice

The claim made for institutional ethnography is that it offers a knowledge resource for people who want to work towards a more equitable society. Its politics are built into its mode of inquiry. It requires taking sides. As we conclude
this book, we want to return to the question that motivated our writing: *can
anyone except technical experts with lengthy scholarly training do institutional ethnography?*
We have shown our hand on this point already. We know that many people who
are attracted to institutional ethnography simply cannot make a commitment to
an extended scholarly career. This book is premised on the belief that institutional ethnography can be made accessible to people who want to use it without
necessarily undertaking a long-term study of its theory and methodology.

As we wrote, we did recognize that we occasionally downplay the difficulty of
the ideas of institutional ethnography. This is an academic text and we have tried
to avoid over-simplifying and condescending to our readers. It is our view that
learning the special language required by a new reader of institutional ethnography should not be daunting even though it does demand some special training.
In introducing some theoretical terms, we wanted to offer some sense of the
theoretical complexity of the methodology and to encourage further reading in
the field. Many who have engaged in this discourse understand how rewarding it
can be. It is also encouraging to know that new ways of teaching institutional
ethnography are being innovated, as successive generations of scholars become
its instructors. At this point it seems appropriate to introduce readers to some
studies that variously trained users of the approach can do and have done.

Studies by Institutional Ethnographers with Research Preparation in Master's Programs

This section contains examples of research conducted by institutional ethnographers after approximately one year or so of Master's level studies – the examples are from a growing list of interesting short scholarly studies. It should be noted that people with similar amounts of training to these writers are also using their institutional ethnographic training every day at work, where it influences how they understand and address practical problems. People working outside of academia rarely have the time or the incentive to write descriptively about their work. For readers of a book like this one, that is a significant loss. In some ways, the following summaries of scholarly research hint at how practitioners in various fields could benefit from having institutional ethnographic skills. In the final section, we turn to institutional ethnography that is even more embedded in practice.

Sonya Jakubec and her Study of Mental Health Care in West Africa

Sonya Jakubec is a nurse who worked with a non-governmental agency in The Gambia for several years in the 1990s, prior to beginning her Master's studies. She came back to university because she was not satisfied that she understood sufficiently her experiences in Africa. Motivated by a commitment to public service and to engaging in development work, she had undertaken a post as a technical advisor to help establish a community mental health program in The Gambia. She found this work personally challenging and gratifying yet it also left her with unanswered questions about her own involvement as well as that of other "outsiders." Her program of studies at the University of Victoria included several courses in institutional ethnography that offered her a way of reflecting analytically on her African experiences. She undertook coursework over twelve months and then began her thesis (2001). She brought her developing analytic interests to her new work as she took up a new position as a faculty member of a Canadian university-college nursing school, one that had a partnership arrangement with an African nursing program. Her study also focused her attention on the global expansion of mental health discourses across groups of clinicians, policymakers, researchers, and international aid specialists.

Her thesis project was an institutional ethnography of a piece of survey research she had conducted in The Gambia. She treated her own experiences as ethnographic data. She writes in an early version of her thesis (Jakubec 2001):

Some accounts of that work are aided by my journal, kept routinely as a method of accounting for my practice. I also relied on photographs that I took documenting how we worked. And I reflected on letters I had sent to friends, family and colleagues back home. These letters became a sort of journal I shared and many of my friends collected them and gave them back to me on my return. These are sources of the experiential data that provide the informal knowing, the knowledge of the everyday, that I have set down in several chapters of this thesis.[11]

In addition to her experiential knowledge, Jakubec had collected other documentary materials from her work in Africa. As she developed a theorized way of analyzing her experiences from studying institutional ethnography, she began to reflect on the "pathways" study she had implemented (with the help of the World Health Organization local office in The Gambia and funding from the Canadian government). She saw that she could treat the survey instrument itself and its antecedents in mental health research as data.

Towards the end of her two-year posting to The Gambia, Jakubec had been struggling to solve the problem of sustainability of the work in which she had been involved there. The work of her community mental health team was flourishing and people who had previously not been receiving attention for mental illness were coming under its care. She wanted to leave with a sense that the work would continue without her. But how would her locally-based team of nurses acquire the supplies that Jakubec had been instrumental in getting from aid agencies, for instance? As she made the rounds to those who had been involved in supplying the community mental health program, she continually heard the refrain "we need more information about mental illness in this country." What puzzled her was that she had been collecting and reporting mental health statistics for two years, and she knew that a study had been conducted for the government by a Nigerian psychiatrist several years previously. What information was needed, she wondered, and why were her reports not sufficient to support her requests? Aid agency staff guided her to possible research tools that they suggested would supply the information to support requests for ongoing financial aid. Thus she found herself implementing a World Health Organization instrument called a "pathways study" in which her team filled out survey forms as they went about their work meeting and interacting with patients across the country.

In her thesis research, Jakubec analyzed the use of this self-study of the mental health care that her team routinely conducted. She analyzed two aspects of it. First, she analyzed the survey's Encounter Form and its use in the field. The Encounter Form was to be filled out as mental health staff "encountered" their patients. It asked them to document the patients' symptoms and propose a diagnosis and a recommended treatment. Jakubec contrasted how her team worked with patients before and during the survey. She argued that their practice changed as they integrated the survey's work process. It nudged the nurses, who were Gambian nationals with some "Western" nursing training, into a stronger sense of professionalism. She saw how doing the survey not only made them value psychiatric treatments over traditional treatments, but the process of documentation in English helped institute a professional status hierarchy for the team over local healers. This self-study, she concluded, was undermining those working relations and as she followed the use of the information gathered, she saw that it would potentially put local healers out of business. This was a problem for many reasons, including, importantly, the highly unreliable access in The Gambia to the pharmaceutical supplies that the study's documentation constituted as professionally correct treatment. Local healers offered help in traditional ways and they often had contracts to supply food and other necessities. Although Jakubec saw that the healers' work need to be supplemented, she was not happy to see it displaced entirely.

The second part of her analysis was conducted as a text-reader conversation. She sought out and reviewed documentary materials that were available to her through the World Health Organization and aid agencies. In her analysis, she read the text of the self-study for its origins in the discourses that she had reviewed and analyzed, following up on language and symbols within the self-study texts themselves. She focused on the notion it carried of a correct pathway of referral of patients to psychiatric practitioners that should be expedited. From the literature on pathways studies, she learned how to interpret the survey's attention to "delay" in referral to psychiatric treatment. She concluded that the study *creates* meanings about mental health treatment in poor countries that call for specific actions – thus articulating with an existing funding agenda. The world mental health framework, Jakubec showed, comes from priorities developed in a coalition of interests expressed in international development, mental health research, global trade arrangements, and so on. From this framework emerge priorities aimed at, for instance, efforts to increase efficiency in reducing the "burden of disease," thus increasing productivity in developing countries. Jakubec concluded that her team's local work was being directed by this ruling framework being imposed from outside. As she worked to support her team's sustainability, the research she implemented advanced this external order. Jakubec began to see this knowledge technology as a feature of modern day colonialism.

This is a sophisticated analysis that offers insight into many of the practical problems that Jakubec (and other international development workers) experience. It answers some of the questions that kept arising as she sought financial and material aid for continuing support of the Gambian program she had been advising. From her analysis, she could see that aid follows a plan that does not necessarily relate to local conditions, needs, and plans. Rather, the master plan arises in conceptual work done elsewhere and, to have her local work supported, she needed to represent it within the terms and criteria of the master plan. This view of aid for mental health is not explicit but operates at the level of discursively-organized ruling relations. The analysis supports Jakubec's own capacity to participate intelligently in such venues as the World Assembly for Mental Health that she had recently attended, a collaborative event coordinated by the World Federation for Mental Health. Here she found the organization and management of global mental health being criticized as well as theorized. Jakubec suggests that her analysis offers a useful critical perspective to complement the recent upsurge of resistance to international aid whose first interest, it is sometimes suggested, is in furthering the aims of Western industry.

Jakubec's research interest grew from learning in coursework that one's experiences hold puzzles that are analytically useful as the basis for research. For her and other students, to research their everyday life offers an opportunity to satisfy their curiosity about aspects of their work worlds that, for the most part, remain both mysterious and frustrating. The feature of the methodology that grabbed Jakubec's attention was what (in technical terms) we call its materialism. As G.W. Smith underlines in his piece on methodology in Campbell and Manicom (1995), institutional ethnography departs from analytic approaches that are speculative in nature by having the researcher find and map the material connections showing the actual social organization of everyday events.

Rena Miller and her "Insider's" Study of Palliative Care

Rena Miller is a social worker whose Master's thesis (1997) is exemplary of how analysis in institutional ethnography can connect personal experiences and their social organization. Towards the end of her graduate studies, her husband, Jim, a Vietnam war veteran, was diagnosed with advanced cancer related to "agent orange" exposure. Rena Miller and her two teenaged sons cared for Jim at home in the few months before he died. Their family doctor and the local health department's palliative care program provided service to the family. Miller kept a personal journal of her experiences and she later applied for, and received, the records of the palliative care intervention from the health department through Freedom of Information processes. These and the public documentary materials of the palliative care program became the basis for the institutional ethnography she conducted after she returned to finish her studies and write a thesis.

Her writing as author/researcher is the intimate and pain-filled account of a woman caring for her dying husband and also a sharply analytic account of that period. Specifically, Miller explores her involvement with the palliative care program and its staff. As primary caregiver to her husband, she was the subject of much of the professional attention that was recorded in the palliative care texts. As an experienced social worker, she recognized the caring efforts being made by the staff but throughout the few months that the service continued, she found herself increasingly at odds with their assessments and interventions and she and her husband finally asked that they no longer visit.

Miller's analysis focused on the texts that documented the palliative care interactions. She read them in the context of other documents – the scholarly literature she reviewed, pamphlets, and a manual on palliative care that were brought into her home. She also read her records within their organizational framing by the agency policies and practices. In addition, she read them as an "insider" to the events that they appeared to chronicle. As Miller reviewed the records of the palliative care team, she saw how she became the focus of a text-mediated work process that identifies a problem that the worker [N] responds to appropriately according to palliative care measures. In an analytic chapter that she entitled "Wife Rena Teary" she analyzes one organizational record called an open flow sheet. She argues that a particular palliative intervention was not orientated to her as a person, but the textual work-up made her into a problem that was manageable, at least from the perspective of the professional. Being objectified in these work processes, she was no longer the subject of what was happening. She offers an insider's account of what objectification feels like.

> [N] continued to work on the problem of "Wife Rena Teary" through two subsequent telephone contacts. On March 6 she started a new open flow sheet without the typed in problem names. She omitted some of the previous categories, and added "General Status" and "Family Coping" as problem names. In the latter box she observed "Rena's OK, but shows stress. Seeing [E] the hospice volunteer today. Jim does not want more people" (Miller 1997, 74).

One week later, March 13, Miller notes her own response to N's recording: "Rena feels better seeing [E]". These notations are puzzling to me except as the representation of work performed to solve a manageable problem of her own construction (Miller 2997, 75).

Miller queried the notion of her tears being represented as "stress." Noting that she cried everyday, she did not recognize this as a problem, certainly not one that needed to be fixed by attending a counsellor. Consulting her own journal she finds that

March 6 was not only the day of my counselling appointment with [E] but also the day that we were setting up a hospital bed in the living room. Jim had become too weak to climb stairs and we had to make the difficult decision to move downstairs ... It was a wrenching loss for both of us to be unable to sleep together... Reviewing the open flow sheet, I realized that what was jarring to me about "Rena's OK but shows stress" was its total separation and distinction from the issue of the hospital bed. In the very first problem category "A[ctivities of] D[aily] L[iving]" [N] wrote on March 6 "Hospital bed being set up". This entry is physically separated from "Family Coping" Nothing links them together on the flow sheet and my perception remains that "hospital bed being set up" was entered as a solution to the manageable problem of Jim's declining strength. To me "hospital bed being set up" *was* a problem: a separation foreshadowing the impending and final separation, and thus an integral part of the huge unresolvable problem of Jim's dying. There's something belittling about seeing this graphically reduced to separate manageable bits in the open flow sheet, something smug and self-serving about the tidy solutions provided for these constructed problems.

The final solution to "Wife Rena teary" is the entry "Rena feels better seeing [E]". Looking at this entry, I once again feel bemused at the way my experience has been altered to appear in this guise. First of all, I found it a challenge to get to see [E]... After our appointment ...[E] went on holiday, and though she did give me her home number, I did not use it. I met her once again sometime after Jim's death; I wasn't "seeing" her regularly as suggested in [N's] note. (Miller 1997, 75-6).

Generally taken for granted by service providers, Miller's analysis reconnects professional interventions with the routine methods of thinking, planning, and recording that stand behind them. She explicates how she was made an appropriate *object* for a course of effective palliative care action through this textual work. Her argument is that this accomplished and displayed, organizationally, a manageable problem being dealt with, although it was not her problem. The open flow sheet's categorizing constituted a distinct and mandated organizational approach to the conduct of palliative care. As such, among other things, it solved communication problems in an agency where staffing was sometimes a problem. For instance, casual staff might be dropped into the roster and the information in the record cued them as to what work to do. In a multidisciplinary team, it is commonplace for records to be used in this way. Miller's point was not that this was unusual but that it did not work in her or her family's interests. Miller deployed her analysis to reflect critically on both personal and professional issues. She says:

> What I learned helped me to dispel, forever I hope, the guilt that dogged my research and made me reluctant to discuss it. I saw that the construction of "palliative care recipients" – a category into which we did not fit properly – was not intended to address individual needs and feelings, but those categorical needs and feelings sanctioned by discourse and amenable to tending by the palliative care team. My discomfort is comprehensible to me as the sense of being squeezed to fit as an object of work into the organizational context ... My analysis also helped me to see how the textually mediated process of helping constructs the workers involved as much as it does the clients or patients. This bridged the gap between my sense of most workers as competent and caring, and my overall experience of being objectified and misinterpreted ... The workers' caring and helpful intentions can be overwhelmed by a process that is unable to address individuality [subjectivity] in any useful way. (Miller 1997, 95-6)

Conducting this analysis helped Miller reflect on and sort out her personal feelings of resentment about the palliative care service into which she was brought as an unwilling subject. Her analysis clarified what had been happening and how it was organized outside of her family's wishes and needs, and perhaps even outside of the workers' intentions. She became clearer about her own critique. That was important in dissolving the sense of guilt that she carried about not being grateful. It was also important to her own professional practice. It supported a growing sense that professionals may over-estimate their usefulness and their capacity to really help others through difficult times. She recognized how organizational features of professional work are, at the very least, likely to undermine good intentions.

Karen Jung and her Study of a University Disability Policy

Jung's Master's thesis (2000) in the University of Victoria's Sociology Department compares disability theory to the theory of institutional ethnography and it explores some of the workings of the university's disability policy. She studied what she called the university's disabilities apparatus, problematizing its notions of "accessibility" and "accommodation" as they are put into practice and operate in the everyday world. She interviewed women students with chronic illnesses and whose disabilities are more or less invisible. About her methodology she says, "Working with an "insider's standpoint" is one of the key features of Smith's sociological enterprise. Here, women are "experts" in their own lives and the everyday world is the world that they experience directly" (Jung 2000, 66)

Following Smith (1987), she reports that she listened to the women students to discover an organizing logic in their talk that is located elsewhere than in their own activity and experience. The interviews became analytically important because "the way that terms are used in their original context, including their syntactic arrangements, is 'controlled' or 'governed' by its social organization and ... the same social organization is present as an ordering procedure in how people tell others about that original setting" (Smith 1987, 188). It was no surprise for her to discover that those interviews revealed how "the chronically ill individual's choices and courses of action become bound up in and shaped by the organizational practices and wider social relations that regulate and organize the experience of illness and disability" (Jung 2000, 67).

To understand her interviews, Jung turned to her research on the policies and practices of the university disabilities apparatus, including the Office of Students with Disabilities and its staff. The Policy for Providing Accommodation to Students with a Disability had been ratified by the governing body of the university in 1997. It outlines the university's moral and legal duty to provide academic accommodation to students such that "fair and consistent treatment of people with disabilities" would ensue (Jung 2000, 90). According to the policy, a disability is institutionally recognizable only if it results in problems of access, requires modifications in regular teaching and evaluation practices (accommodation), and is medically verifiable. Accommodation is the institutional response to a student's request. Accommodation, as institutional policy, means granting of extra time to complete assignments, use of special technology, or a variety of other alternations in instructional practices. Any accommodation must conform to academic principles and not cause the university "undue hardship" (92).

Jung found a prevailing idea of "unfair advantage" evoked by the granting of accommodation to students with disabilities. She heard it first in her interviews with women students. In the following excerpt, one student explains:

> so first of all I went to the Grad Advisor and appealed to her on the basis of my disability. What I said was – I have a chronic illness … I have a disability of pace, and I need you to recognize that and treat me equitably. And what I got back was a line about – well, we need to create a level playing field. And I said to her – when you live with a disability there is no level playing field … I do not want fairness, I want equity. And she did not understand the difference. She kept falling back on – we have to treat everyone the same, we have to be fair to the other students as well. (105)

Jung discovered the idea of unfair advantage embedded in the talk of the Coordinator of the Office of Students with Disabilities whose responsibility it is to implement the policy. She points out that he also took for granted the prevailing view that making accommodation for students with a disability lowers academic standards and also that professors are right to assume there will be some cheating in relation to claims of disability. Medical validation of disability is required to offset such views. Jung also described the rather extensive work associated with an application for accommodation – work that must be done by the individual students making the claim. They must learn to cast themselves into the categories and terms of the disabilities policy, and conform to important features of the university and its instructional programs and practices. They must confront and deal with the (properly) skeptical professor and satisfy his demand for evidence. Jung's analysis showed how this constructs the student as a creature of the policy. She explains that the chronically ill women who were in a position to claim accommodation "took up a subject position from within the ruling relations of the university" (Jung 2001, 112). For instance, they often said that they felt guilty and unsure of the appropriateness of their request for accommodation. Besides accounting for the women's skeptical self-appraisal, Jung concluded that the accommodation work serves to protect the institution from "wear and tear" on its taken-for-granted values, beliefs, and practices. She argues that, by having the Office, the Policy, and students engaging in requests for accommodation, the University is fulfilling its legal and moral requirements.

In her words: "[In] requesting accommodation, regardless of whether or not [it] is useful, or [even if] the individual drops the request, … the chronically ill student is always participating in the realization of an institutional course of action that "counts' on behalf of the university's public display of good citizenship" (119).

Her analysis speaks of the ways that a policy works for some individuals and offers some insights into how and why, in some cases, it does not work. In doing so, it illuminates the actualities of policy implementation, showing it as organizationally-specific methods of interpretive practice involving people from its being established in text to how it plays out in real lives. In making this analysis of a small group of chronically ill students, Jung has managed to draw out a critical analysis that has a general and generalizable character. A disability policy in another institution might be found to work the same way. The social relations Jung mapped are general. Institutional ethnography's explication, in this case of organizational relations of ruling, supports knowledge claims of this sort.

Practising a Sociology for People

In proposing and teaching institutional ethnography, Smith's motivation was to create a sociology for people to help them understand the conditions of their oppression. In various ways throughout this book we have noted the contradiction between the highly technical practice of institutional ethnography and the needs of people to understand their own lives. The contradiction is real. Because the social organization of everyday life is complex, so are the methods of analysis that can adequately address its complexity. Institutional ethnography has become a scholarly undertaking. As such, people who can practise this theoretically challenging work are those who have scholarly careers offering them sufficient research time. Also, the complexity of the research often overwhelms the researcher's intention to make the analysis available in forms that people can use for changing their lives. Institutional ethnographers struggle constantly with this contradiction.

The student work discussed above shows how the politics of knowing has emerged as central to their studies. Conducting such studies will change the ways that these student-researchers work in the future, no matter what their undertakings. The work we turn to now springs from a different set of locations. Some institutional ethnographers conduct their research within activist situations, where it is part of how they are learning to think out a direction for change. The summaries in this section are of three analyses made by institutional ethnographers exemplifying work that has been motivated by and/or implicated in this kind of ongoing practical project. Roxana Ng's important study of women's community work is presented first. It was conducted while Ng was involved in a setting established by activists to place immigrant women in paid jobs. It is followed by a description of how Marie Campbell has attempted to adapt institutional ethnography for use in a participatory research project, involving people with disabilities and health care providers. Finally, we discuss Gary Kinsman's reflections on being a political-activist ethnographer during his own extended career in community-based gay-rights activism, in this case around AIDS treatments.

Roxana Ng's Study of a Job Placement Agency for Immigrant Women

Roxana Ng's study is published as *The Politics of Community Services: Immigrant Women, Class and State* (1996). The PhD research on which this book is based was conducted in the 1980s (first published 1988) but its analysis stands up well across the years and it was revised for a second edition in 1996. Community workers who encounter the book often recognize the issues being discussed from having lived through a similar situation. The story goes like this: local efforts to address a set of problems that people experience lead to community-based action that brings attention to the issue; some sort of institutionalization of services follows and then, to everybody's chagrin, the good work begins to fall apart. Ng conducted ethnographic fieldwork as she volunteered in a community agency that had been formed to help immigrant women find meaningful work. Ng encountered and writes about efforts and successes, as well as tensions and contradictions. Her institutional ethnography describes and analyzes what was happening. She explicates the ruling processes that entered the agency and disorganized its work, as government funding became its modus operandi. Ng analyzes everyday operations of the agency and counsellors' relations among themselves and their women clients and with the employers whose jobs they were filling, but she also introduces some important theoretical discussion. For instance, she offers some insights into how to properly conceptualize the state and its operations. Her account of state funding, for instance, shows how people participate in the ruling relations that subordinate local efforts. She uses the differences in class, gender, race, and ethnicity that her ethnography exposes to make an argument against assumptions that the state operates in the interests of all citizens.

Ng's argument is made though her analysis of the various actual processes of the organization of the agency whereby the state's ruling interests dominate efforts to help immigrant women find suitable paid work. The book traces the sequence of events that brought the activist group of women to the point where they first incorporated their society officially as part of making their efforts fundable. Then they learned that they had to address as a first priority the accountability that government funding brings. Text-mediated processes began to shape the agency's everyday work. For instance, they began to count and report the number of women placed in jobs. This recording came back to haunt them as numbers became treated as evidence of success, superceding the workers' and women's concerns about the jobs. Ng's analysis of the funding and accountability processes shows how they reordered almost everything about the internal relations among the activist workers. But Ng argues that these processes were not taken seriously by the agency as (dis)organizing what was happening. The work of keeping records became a specialized function of one member of the group, who had previously coordinated the counselling work. It absorbed more and more time, and its importance in comparison to counselling grew. In addition, the workers began to see their clients through the perspective provided in the categories of the government's accountability system. Ng writes that

> the way in which ruling processes penetrated the internal operation of the agency was not merely through a direct imposition of directives on its mode of operation. More profoundly, as the employment agency expanded and its functions grew in complexity, a set of new accounting procedures (of clients, of employers, of services provided, etc.) also became the internal requirement of the agency itself. The notion of what counted as proper accounting was one shared by [the government program] and members of the agency. In the course of its development, the perspective of the agency shifted from one which attended to the lived experiences of the clients to the perspective of an impersonal institutional order. (Ng 1996, 46)

This institutional view of the work had important repercussions on the relations among people in the agency. Work with and for clients suffered as counsellors learned that the agency's very existence depended on producing good statistical results. Clients' visits and their expectations about being placed in a good job and treated equitably in their workplaces eventually became a hindrance to getting the agency work done efficiently. For instance, when Ng was being trained to do placement counselling, she was instructed by the coordinator that the client is usually given five chances before her file is closed. That is, she will be referred to five places ... to see if she wants to take the job. In cases where it is "her fault", i.e., if she fails to show up for an interview; if she is too picky about what she wants to do, ...she is only given three chances.... The coordinator explained that, as much as they would like to, they cannot spend all their time with one client. (Ng 1996, 65)

This suggests how the counsellors began to treat clients with increased objectivity, rather than as individuals. Clients' individual circumstances would have been important to how they presented themselves as potential employees – going to jobs that were usually minimum wage, living in the conditions they faced as immigrants possibly difficulty getting around the city or accessing child care. But the counselling work was becoming secondary to the requirements for management – especially reporting of placement rates – of the agency. Tensions among staff, and between the staff and the board, also mounted. Ng's study offers readers a good sense of how institutional ethnography can be a resource for activists who find themselves in these kinds of contradictory situations. Her analysis shows how these tensions, disagreements and the loss of focus on the original advocacy goals arose directly from specific organizational processes. In one example, the emphasis on generating placement rates created competitiveness among the staff. Ng explains:

When ... job openings became scarce, counsellors began to keep their own files ... Instead of filing the order in the agency's job order file, (a counsellor) kept it for her clients ... Here we see the way in which a collective effort on behalf of labour became individualized: In order to maintain their own placement rates and protect their own clients, counsellors began to carry out their work in relation to their own gains within the agency. (Ng 1996, .82)

Rather than proposing a general stance towards state funding and community activism, Ng promotes a careful analytic understanding of any particular situation. She says, "an in-depth grasp of the financial and budgetary processes is essential for groups to discover how to work creatively while relying on state funding" (Ng 1996, 93). Ng has set out a clear and detailed method in her book for grasping the ruling effects of organizational arrangements on the people, the work, the working relations and the outcomes of activist community work. In opening up for critical analysis routine activities that appear to be simply administrative, this study has wide-ranging implications for all sorts of human service work as well as activist undertakings.

A Collaborative Study: *Project Inter-Seed*

Marie Campbell had the opportunity to work with a community group that wanted to research a problem its members had described. Invited to consult with the group, she listened to their ideas and needs, and then sketched a possible research project the conceptual foundation of which was institutional ethnography. Project Inter-Seed (Campbell, Copeland and Tate, 1999) was planned to be participatory; that is, it was to be conducted in a manner that kept the goals of the project and the research itself in the hands of a research team that included members of the community group. Some predictable challenges arose about the extent to which, in institutional ethnography, control of the research can be shared authentically. Unlike Participatory Action Research, where the methodology relies on participants directing the course of the research, this inquiry's institutional ethnographic methodology remained central to the project. That is perhaps the most interesting feature to explore here, in a book about institutional ethnography.

The project, as it was described in funding proposals (written by Campbell), was to explore health care, problems experienced by people with disabilities who were living in the community of Greater Victoria.[12] The funding efforts themselves established certain relations among the players in the project that challenged its participatory character. For instance, to access a community-based research funding program the applicant had to provide evidence of community partnerships in place. As already mentioned, preliminary work had been carried out to develop a partnership between Campbell and the Disability Resource Centre of South Vancouver Island, whose members had been instrumental in promoting the idea of research. But the funding of Project Inter-Seed as scholarly research brought into the relationship ruling relations, beginning with the university, where Campbell was a faculty member, and its financial management. The various funding sources that were tapped each demanded a certain work-up of the topic and certain forms of accountability. Although the project came from grassroots beginnings, the funding went mainly to the principal investigator, as is the routine practice of scholarly grants programs. As accountability became the responsibility of the principal investigator, it was turned over to the staff she hired as the project was put into place — with an office, equipment, modes of communication, record-keeping etc.[13] All this work of establishing the project helped to impose certain relations of ruling.

Yet, there was a commitment to take seriously the participation of those who are usually thought of (and treated as) the subjects of the research. Participant involvement, however, was never straightforward or unproblematic. The project never really looked the way the literature on participatory research said it should. The principal investigator carried the designated responsibility, not just for managing the funding but also for the project's scholarly rigour. To fulfill all these responsibilities, staff made certain decisions without the participation of the partners and throughout the course of the project, carried out certain tedious but necessary tasks. While this division of responsibility and labour is standard research practice, it contravenes tenets of participatory research. Yet another practicality intervened in the original intention to do participatory research. To get the project going, the staff recruited and conducted initial interviews with people with disabilities who volunteered to tell their stories about their experiences with health care. This method of recruitment brought people with disabilities into the project as paid participants, but only after several months of the project's operation. For all these reasons, it seemed more realistic to use the term *collaborative* rather than participatory to describe the research process.

These constraints aside, the research team was built up from people with disabilities whose lives provided them with expertise on the nature of the topic being studied.[14] As the project developed, people from the different locations in the community assumed relevant positions in the research team and its advisory committee. Health care agencies played important roles in the research, offering access to observational sites, for instance. Their members also joined the research team. The researchers with disabilities were involved in selecting applicants from health care agencies who were being seconded to the research team. From their early learning about the research, the researchers with disabilities helped "train" the health care provider team members. In the course of these efforts, working relations were established in the manner that participatory research sees as beneficial — everyday issues of power and authority became the topic of discussion. Research team tasks included work on resolving conflicts and reasserting the primacy of the goal of this inquiry to take the standpoint of people with disabilities.[15] Eventually, dissemination of results became a shared task with team members taking the roles in which they felt capable.

While the contradictions of doing institutional ethnography as collaborative research are many, so are the benefits. In Project Inter-Seed, once the methodology of institutional ethnography was introduced, the team could begin to explore how appropriate it was to their needs. Theorizing the research was a matter of conceptualizing how this project would identify things that were important to team members' lives. The use of institutional ethnography was debated within the group and accepted as coherent with the values of the project that also included the tenets of independent living and the principles of community development. Through this debate, the delivery of home support services to research subjects was chosen as the research focus. Data collection and analysis relied on team members grasping the crucial theoretical notions, for instance, of social relations. In observations, interviews, and the collection of relevant documents, team members captured accounts of health care in process. The team met regularly and reviewed and debated what they saw in the transcripts of data that had been circulated to them. Multiple perspectives became an everyday occurrence in these discussions. The notion, from institutional ethnography, that a knower's location in the world provides the basis for what can be seen and understood was useful for sorting out and understanding differences in team members' perspectives. So was the grounding premise of the research — that is, that the study was being conducted to discover how certain features of the lives of people with disabilities were organized. While an agency's, or a health care worker's, practices might be explained and legitimized by ruling organizational policies and so on, the team recognized that the purpose of the research was to identify how those practices actually impacted on people's lives. Thus, the authority for interpreting an observation would shift away from a ruling perspective. The whole team had to learn how to take the standpoint of people with disabilities. From those analytic efforts everyone saw that things look different from different positions and they began to accept that much in the health care world is not organized to reflect, acknowledge or make use of the experiences of people with disabilities. This was perhaps the most useful insight for ongoing work to address problems.

While a number of reports were written, conference presentations made, papers published, and consultations held with organizations, managers and policymakers, the outcome of the research that has attracted the most positive response is a board game that the research team developed.[16] The game incorporates into cards what the team members learned from their research experience. Called "Ain't Life Ducky?" the game offers players the opportunity to experience vicariously what a person with a disability lives through. Sometimes players must make a choice or a decision, sometimes they are simply given a problem that, because it interferes with their life, interrupts their progress in the game. As the game is played, the educational aim is to discuss and debate the (social organization of) incidents, circumstances, and feelings invoked by the cards a player pulls. The game has been situated within a workshop offered to health care providers, policy-makers, respite workers, people with disabilities, volunteers and staff in advocacy and support agencies, and students in nursing and social work classes. Players reflect on whatever ideas they may carry about living with a disability. For instance, health care professionals may be judgemental of clients with disabilities, seeing them as angry or uncooperative and difficult. Or people with disabilities may blame the bad attitudes of professionals for what happens to them. In either case, individuals – whether the person with a disability, a family member or a professional – are often considered to be the problem. The game introduces a method of making other sorts of connections. For people who need to navigate through the often troubled waters of living in a world built for non-disabled people, the game offers useful new ways of seeing things. The research on which the game is based offers a basic mapping of some of the social relations of community service delivery that, when opened up through discussion, lead to new insights.

One contribution that Project Inter-Seed makes to thinking about participatory research is in suggesting how to think about efforts to "democratize" the relations of research. Because an institutional ethnography framework conceptualizes the relations between society, individuals and institutions in a particular manner, that framework must guide data collection and analysis. That theoretical-methodological commitment limits the full play of equality among team members. The research team proposed an alternative view of equitable relations that assumes that members play different roles and contribute different kinds of valued expertise. However, the knowledge being generated was always an explanation and expression of the standpoint of people with disabilities. The way the study was conceptualized meant that all the researchers learned to do this self-consciously. Institutional ethnography built into the inquiry and the findings the centrality and valuing of the standpoint of the subjects of the research.

Gary Kinsman's Writing from Inside Political Activism

In the article summarized here, Gary Kinsman speaks about himself as a political-activist ethnographer who was working in AIDS activism from the late 1980s to the 1990s (Kinsman 1997). He also reveals himself as an historian writing the history of important strands of this work as it looks from the standpoint of the activist. His is an alternative account in which, as institutional ethnographer, he exposes the ruling relations as he came to know them from inside a social movement. He examines texts of important policies that came to organize the everyday work of community-based organizations. He and his colleagues organized and attended meetings, listened to speeches, criticized drafts of policy papers, wrote and presented briefs — all of which he recognizes as having a contradictory character. On the one hand, like those activists before them and those following after them, they made demands on the state for an adequate response to the AIDS crisis on behalf of people who had individual needs. They worked in various ways to make these demands heard. On the other hand, Kinsman draws on G.W. Smith (1989), Roxana Ng (1996), and others to show how working in relation to state initiatives pulls a social movement into the state's agenda. This article published in Bill Carroll's 1997 collection *Organizing Dissent: Contemporary Social Movements in Theory and Practice*, focuses on Kinsman's explication of some of those processes of incorporation and regulation. In particular, he chronicles the state's use of consultation that over the years became known as "partnership" and he analyzes and criticizes the way that official policies make use of the concept of "responsibility."

Kinsman's account situates his inquiry's "orienting question" in "an experience of rupture between the needs of community based AIDS organizing and state and other professional regulatory practices on the federal and provincial levels" (Kinsman 1997, 215). In reviewing how a national and a provincial AIDS strategy had been put in place, he sees gains and losses for activists and their concerns about people infected with HIV. For example, AIDS activism has fallen off, as community groups take up the provision of services to people living with AIDS and HIV for which state funding has been made available. In another contradictory turn of events, he notes that the Krever Commission's [17] inquiry into tainted blood has offered the media the notion of "innocent" and "guilty" AIDS victims. He recognizes that AIDS activism has the added task of countering the divisions created between the different groups — those infected by the blood supply and others infected through sexual activities and intravenous drug use (220). As an activist, he must be concerned about the financial implications that this distinction carries. He knows that everyone living with AIDS and HIV requires financial and social support.

These are his observations. His analysis attempts to locate the ruling practices that shaped the events in which he and his colleagues participated Using an institutional ethnographic approach, he turns to the official texts of the various AIDS strategy documents. He wants to "recover part of the work process that went into the formation of the [national and provincial AIDS] strateg[ies]" (Kinsman 1997, 220). His analytic process is to read the documents and account for his interpretation by referencing his insider knowledge of how they related to what was actually happening. A few examples show how he used his insider reading.

Focusing on the use by both the federal and provincial governments of consultation with stakeholders, he questions the notion of "partnership" that became a prominent feature of the consultation. Partnerships offered activists a place for asserting their interests, Kinsman claims, referencing his own work in Nova Scotia at the time:

taking advantage of the rhetoric of 'partnership', and the government's commitment to it, we were able to make advances when we had a clearly defined agenda and were able to seize the dynamic of consultation ... Unfortunately there were also points of division in the coalition, including questions about how accommodating to be with the government. The government was also able to use the rhetoric of "consultation" and "partnership" against us by emphasizing the atmosphere of compromise and [consensus] while also talking about financial constraints. (Kinsman 1997, 225)

However helpful it was to be treated as a partner in developing state policy, the language of partnership obscured how the different participants understood and defined the needs that the partnerships were to address. It also obscured the underlying differences in the social power and interests of those involved. Activists representing people whose lives depended upon the decisions and actions coming out of the AIDS strategy became just one partner among many. Kinsman found that his and his colleagues' expertise was routinely subordinated in dialogue that privileged the views of partners with professional knowledge, for instance. He also saw that the relations between profit-oriented drug companies and governments were being conceived within the same general terminology of partnership. Partnership arrangements shifted the ground of a terrain of struggle over proper treatments and public responsibility. Under the partnership rubric and work processes, the state could manage more successfully their response to AIDS and AIDS-related demands of activists. Kinsman found that the national AIDS strategy expresses a "neutral stance" in which the state appears to stand above competing interest groups (Kinsman 1997, 227). While a neutral and professional framing of AIDS work reduced some of the tensions that activists might otherwise have created, it did not eliminate the denigration of HIV-infected people. They were constructed as the "risk" and the "problem" (229). Kinsman emphasizes the trouble with that formulation, recognizing how it fails to recognize a direction for public policy initiatives such as educational campaigns. "The framing defines the issue as their responsibility not to engage in risk activities, even though the vast majority of HIV transmission occurs from people who have no knowledge they are HIV+ or are ignorant of how it is transmitted" (229-30).

Kinsman's analysis of language draws readers' attention to how AIDS is named in official documents. He points out that since the early 1990s, the official language has shifted from calling AIDS a fatal illness to calling it a chronic, manageable disease or condition. Even that term has been useful for the state's management of its problem in regulating the response to AIDS and AIDS activism.

> Originally, this term was developed from the standpoints of AIDS activists and PLWA/HIVs [people living with AIDS and HIV infection] to get at the state, professional, and pharmaceutical practices that block access to needed treatments ... Now it has been turned and shifted by some medical and government officials: [it] has become a "chronic manageable condition", but without the state, medical, and corporate blockages being substantially addressed ... The state and professions give individuals the responsibility for managing their own health but do not give them the resources, supports, or knowledge to do this. <Kinsman, 1997, 230-1>

He draws on instances when activist groups have been funded to provide services to people living with AIDS and HIV and have given up dissent. He points out how funding this work has helped the state solve its problems of governing, even as it begins to address, albeit inadequately, activists' concerns.

Kinsman's writing draws us, as readers, into the story he is telling so that we can see what he and his colleagues see, and from their perspectives. The events that he describes as history and those going on at the time of the writing (and being dissected by him) are elements of a struggle. He shows how texts are part of the struggle. Writing about political action gives the paper its particular character and structure. It is not written with the ordinary and expected structure of a scholarly essay with an argument supported by data that have been collected for that expository purpose. This article is an account of a political campaign that is in the process of being waged, with some results now emerging more or less clearly. Other observations are still being worked with, and their meanings to the campaign still being discovered. Kinsman's writing brings us into this struggle – we are readers whom he instructs on how to read events as he does. Politically engaged, this article does not have tidy conclusions, but instead poses questions that remain to be answered.

Analyzing events that are unfolding as one writes is not easy. It is quite a different matter from testing a hypothesis, applying a theory to data that "stand still". Yet, this kind of on-the-go analysis is what a social movement needs. It is an account that can be corrected when a new piece of information is uncovered or a different public response occurs. Activism is work toward a more equitable society that institutional ethnography claims to support. It is a good note to end on, a place that institutional ethnographers want to inhabit.

Subverting Institutionalization

This book's goal has been to explain as succinctly as possible how to conduct institutional ethnography. We have presented what we think one needs to know in order to begin and carry out research in this mode. That includes touching on the theory upon which the method relies. In this chapter's examples of institutional ethnography, readers can see the methodology implemented across a variety of sites. A range of topics, approaches to data collection and analysis, and findings are displayed. Each analyst explicates ruling relations that organize the situation studied, exposing how ruling texts are activated by those involved. When the presentation of the analysis is sufficiently clear, we can all see how things have happened as they did. Most importantly, the structure of the analytic account expresses a different standpoint from that of the ruling texts. The research takes a standpoint in the everyday world and of people whose lives are subordinated to ruling practices.

To conclude this chapter, and the book, we want to draw readers' attention to what Dorothy Smith has called the subversion of institutionalization that is possible through knowledge constructed from a non-ruling place. At the end of her *Everyday World as Problematic* (1987) Smith sounds a warning about the methods she has posited there. She declares that

> they [the methods] must be anchored in relations connecting them with women who do not participate in the relations of ruling and the discourses that interpenetrate them. The critical force of these methods is contained and "institutionalized" if they are not articulated to relations creating

124

linkages outside and beyond the ruling apparatus, giving voice to women's experience, opening up to women's gaze the forms and relations organizing women' lives, and enlarging women's powers and capacities to organize in struggle against the oppression of women. (Smith 1987, 225)

Smith speaks of women's experience and women's lives here but, as we have seen here, her methods can be applied to all those who stand in similar relations to ruling. What Smith saw about developing knowledge from a standpoint in women's experience remains the key to doing social analysis on behalf of those whom ruling relations subjugate. Her reminder here is that a method of inquiry is not magic. She means that knowledge is not transformative in and of itself. Rather, she instructs that "connections have to be made such that we who are doing the technical work of research and explication are responsible in what we write *to those for whom we write* (Smith 1987, 224, emphasis added).

To explore this responsibility to those for whom we write, we can return to the examples of institutional ethnographies selected for inclusion in this chapter. For whom did Sonya Jakubec, Rena Miller or Karen Jung write besides their thesis committees? To whom (else) are they responsible? How? If we are to take seriously such socially demanding expectations, how can they apply to students' work? How can Smith's view of research that subverts institutionalization be taught? To consider questions such as these, it may help to reflect on how the analysts appearing in this chapter were orientated to the subjects of their research and to others who might find it useful.

Jakubec's story earlier in the chapter hints at her discovery of an increasingly vocal resistance that is mounting to international development efforts that do not adequately address local interests. As we read her analysis, we can begin to see how dominant Western ideas, and even needs of donors and donor countries, are built into the conceptualizations of aid and its implementation. She explains how an apparently neutral self-study that she conducted perpetuates ruling relations. Presenting her analysis in international forums is one way that she acts responsibly in Smith's terms. But her involvement in nursing in Africa did not end when she completed her contract as an advisor to the mental health project in The Gambia. She carries with her now her own understanding of how things work as a nursing instructor preparing Canadian nursing students for field visits to Africa. Her study can become a teaching tool. It problematizes experiences in Africa that these privileged Canadians are likely to overlook — unless they develop a specific orientation to them. Jakubec's analysis explicates the ruling relations of that setting. The question of ruling practices that masquerade as development is very difficult to pry apart from the ideology of caring that motives nurses. Those who experience it can feel the contradictions. Teaching from her analysis of such contradictory experiences is another important way that Jakubec is putting her study into practice.

At first glance, Rena Miller's study seems completely focused on an analysis of her personal story. Institutional ethnography can be useful as such and Miller explains how liberating it was for her to come to terms with her own experiences and feelings that had seemed inappropriate. She had found it difficult even to speak about this with her friends. Seeing the textual and organizational structuring of the situations that had aroused her resentment alleviated her guilt about those kinds of responses. Miller's work explored very intimate feelings but her findings of organizational relations of ruling within professional practice can, of course, be generalized beyond her own situation. Now, as an instructor of social work students, she is able to draw on this analysis to address a variety of issues embedded in professional practice and its routine organization. Debates about "who knows what?" and "what status can be claimed for professional expertise?" are highly relevant to the training of all human service workers. Her social work colleagues know her work and value it. Although Miller has not yet published her analysis, it circulates as a thesis, providing the analytic basis for a challenge to everyday assumptions about professionalism. She says that when students see a problem they are likely to feel secure in seeing its solution as the provision of more of their own services. Miller continually places such discussions within the power relations of professional practice, asking her students to treat their ideas as tentative, always opening a place for people's own wishes about their lives.

Institutional ethnographers often recognize that their conversations with informants accomplish more than data collection. Particularly, those institutional ethnographers who are engaged in activism know that their political work is advanced as they also collect data, or so G.W. Smith (1990) has said. The talk in such settings may be mutually informative. Gary Kinsman collects data while he is a participant in activist undertakings. In these types of ethnographic involvement with informants, there is potential for exploring together the relations of ruling that are operating in a setting. But Karen Jung, like many other institutional ethnographers, has a more conventional research relationship with informants. In assessing the impact of her analysis, Jung points out that at the time that she was interviewing women students who were chronically ill, she still did not understand the university's disability policy. She discovered that her informants held a variety of perspectives on their own relation to the policy. They might have been actively involved with the university disability apparatus but, for the most part, these students were not curious about it in the way that she was. It was some time after her interviewing that she began to recognize how the university's ruling relations are built into the policy. She began to see how it operates on the idea of a typical person with a disability and, when a chronically ill woman relates to the university within its terms and practices, she is brought into conformity with that stereotype. This generates the experience of being constructed as "disabled" and it has a variety of consequences, some potentially helpful, some definitely not. Making this analysis available to a constituency of people who can use it happens for Jung, sometimes informally. For example, as she meets women with chronic illnesses who are going back to university and are confronting problems, she discusses what she knows. Jung has also used established methods of scholarly publishing to present this. However it is imparted, Jung's analysis is responsible to those students who find themselves ruled, or potentially so, in such relations.

The research projects by Ng, Campbell et al., and Kinsman were selected for this chapter because they each present work pitched towards community purposes. How these researchers have approached their work seems entirely different, one from the others. The approaches are similar in maintaining a critical analytical focus on the relations that rule people's lives. Ng's book is now well known and is widely used in university classes where instructors and students treat it not only as an exemplary description of institutional ethnography, but also as illustrative of problems likely to be faced in community work. Its insights are useful in a practical way. Its clarity makes it accessible for people from many backgrounds. The value of clear writing as an important political element of a researcher's responsibility should not be underestimated. The Campbell et al. account attempts to make institutional ethnography available for use by community members with varying backgrounds, and not necessarily with any research training. Absorbing the methodology was a challenge within the project, but it supplied a solid core for the work that allowed the researchers to discover important features of how health services worked (or did not) for people with disabilities. The community work it spawned continues, with people taking it forward in various ways. Perhaps that is a sufficient measure of its success. Kinsman's research is conducted on activism in which he is participating. He does not tell us, in the piece summarized, how much his analyzes are used within this movement, if at all. Yet he seems to be writing to colleagues, more than to academics. Explicating the discourses of public policy as practical activity seems to approach Smith's point about subverting institutionalization. She suggests that our texts should work for people outside ruling positions, to help them recognize their own participation in the relations that rule them.

Much more could be said about an institutional ethnographer's responsibility to write for people, and to make workable analyses available and accessible to those who need to understand various forms of domination and subordination. These discussions would always have a different character from the discussions about research dissemination among mainstream researchers. For instance, health researchers worry about "research up-take"(Lomas 1997) and extensive strategies are developed to encourage practitioners to use research findings (Mykhalovskiy 2001). That sort of up-take of research results is ruling activity, with new findings being absorbed into a ruling discourse and ruling practices. The responsibility for those in charge of health care and its resources is to get practitioners to implement the recommended approaches that, in our terms, would be called the ruling ideas. The methods proposed in this book, however, allow us to make analyses (texts) that work differently from the ruling texts we analyze. These findings will never form the basis of objective rules, but rather will inform critical analyzes of ruling practices. Where necessary, our studies will help to disclose how objective rules fail when they suppress subjectivity. There is a commitment to making the conditions of people's everyday lives known and knowable as the basis for action. Rather than supporting a ruling perspective and approach, the new institutional ethnographic knowledge should help to form a subject's political consciousness related to equitable decision making, undermining subordination, and so on. We take this to be a serious and valuable contribution.

But Smith warns that "such strategies themselves become merely academic if they are contained within the relations of academic discourse, even a feminist [or other critical] discourse" (Smith 1987, 224). It remains a challenge to institutional ethnographers to avoid becoming institutionalized themselves, drawn into the ruling relations of discourses organized by one class, one gender or sexual orientation, or one race. That is the institutionalization that we want to help subvert. Some of us will be activists, some of us will not. But we all have a social responsibility. Our responsibility is to make texts that express the standpoint of people and to help make them available to those who will use the work's subversive capacity in their own struggles.

References

Becker, Howard, "Whose Side Are We On?" *Social Problems*, Vol.14, 1967, pp.139-247.

Bell, Nancy, *A Child's "Terminal Illness": An Analysis of Text Mediated Knowing*, unpublished Master of Arts thesis, Faculty of Human and Social Development, University of Victoria, 2001.

Campbell, Marie, "Textual Accounts, Ruling Action: The Intersection of Power and Knowledge in the Routine Conduct of Community Nursing Work" *Studies in Cultures, Organizations and Societies*, Vol. X (forthcoming).

——"Participatory Research on Health Care for People with Disabilities: Exploring the Social Organization of Service Provision", *Research In Social Science and Disabilities*, Vol. 1. No. 1, 2000, pp. 131-54.

——"Knowledge, Gendered Subjectivity and Restructuring of Health Care: The Case of the Disappearing Nurse", in S. Neysmith (ed.), *Restructuring Caring Labour: Discourse and State Practice and Everyday Life* (Toronto: Oxford University Press, 2000), pp. 186-208.

——"Institutional Ethnography and 'Experience' as Data" *Qualitative Sociology*, Vol. 21, No. 1, 1998, pp. 55-73.

——"The Structure of Stress in Nurses' Work", in S. Bolaria and H. Dickenson (eds.) *Sociology of Health, Illness and Health Care in Canada*, (Toronto: Harcourt Brace Jovanovich, 1988 and 1994), pp. 592-608.

——Brenda Copeland and Betty Tate with the Research Team, *Project Inter-Seed: Learning From the Health Care Experiences of People with Disabilities*, Final Research Report, University of Victoria, 30 November 1999.

——Brenda Copeland and Betty Tate, "Taking the Standpoint of People with Disabilities in Research: Experiences with Participation" *Canadian Journal of Rehabilitation*, Vol. 12, No. 2, 1998, pp. 95-104.

——and Nancy Jackson, "Learning to Nurse: Plans, Accounts and Action", *Qualitative Health Research* , Vol. 2, No. 4, pp. 475-96.

——and Ann Manicom, *Knowledge, Experience and Ruling Relations: Studies in the Social Organization of Knowledge*, Toronto: University of Toronto Press, 1995.

Carroll, William K. (ed.), *Organizing Dissent: Contemporary Social Movements in Theory and Practice*, Toronto: Garamond Press, 1997.

Chambon, Adrienne, "Foucault's Approach: Making the Familiar Visible", in A Chambon, A. Irving and L. Epstein, (eds.), *Reading Foucault for Social Work*, New York: Columbia University Press, 1999, pp. 51-81.

Cocks, E. and J. Cockram, The Participatory Research Paradigm and Intellectual Disability, *Mental Handicap Research*, Vol. 8, No. 1, 1995, pp. 25-37.

Darville, Richard, "Literacy, Experience, Power", in M. Campbell and A. Manicom (eds.) *Knowledge, Experience and Ruling Relations: Studies in the Social Organization of Knowledge* (Toronto: University of Toronto Press, 1995), pp. 249-261.

De Montigny, Gerald, *Social Working: An Ethnography of Front-line Practice*, Toronto: University of Toronto Press, 1995.

DeVault, Marjorie, *Liberating Method: Feminism and Social Research*, Philadelphia: Temple University Press, 1999.

——and Liza McCoy, Institutional Ethnography: Using Interviews to Investigate Ruling Relations, in J. Gubrium and J. Holstein (eds.), *Handbook of Interview Research: Context and Method* (Thousand Oaks, CA: Sage Publications, 2002), pp. 751-76.

Denzin, Norman, *The Research Act: A Theoretical Introduction to Sociological Methods*, New York: McGraw-Hill, 1978

Diamond, Timothy, *Making Grey Gold: Narratives of Nursing Home Care*, Chicago: University of Chicago Press, 1992.

Fetterman, David, *Ethnography: Step by Step*, Newbury Park, CA: Sage, 1989

Foucault, Michel, *The Order of Things: An Archeology of the Human Sciences*, London: Tavistock, 1970.

——*Power/Knowledge: Selected Interviews and Other Writings, 1972-1977*, New York: Pantheon Books, 1984.

Freire, Paolo, *Pedagogy of the Oppressed*, New York: Herder and Herder, 1972.

Garfinkel, Harold, *Studies in Ethnomethodology*, Englewood Cliffs, New Jersey: Prentice-Hall, 1967.

——Michael Lynch, and Eric Livingston, "The Work of a Discovering Science Constructed with Materials from the Optically Discovered Pulsar," *Philosophy of the Social Sciences*, vol. 11, 1981, pp. 131-58.

Gaventa, J., Participatory Research in North America." *Convergence*, Vol.21, No. 2/3, 1988, pp.19-28.

Giltrow, Janet, *Academic Writing: Writing and Reading Across the Disciplines*, Peterborough, Ontario: Broadview Press, 1995.

Glazer, Barney and Anselm Strauss, *The Discovery of Grounded Theory: Strategies for Qualitative Research*, New York: Aldine, 1967.

Gregor, Frances M., "Nurses' Informal Teaching Practices: Their Nature and Impact on the Production of Patient Care", *International Journal of Nursing Studies*, Vol.38, 2001, pp. 461-70.

——*The Social Organization of Nurses' Educative Work*. Unpublished Doctoral Dissertation, Dalhousie University, Halifax, 1994.

——Factors Affecting the Use of Self-instructional Material by Patients with Ischemic Heart Disease. *Patient Education and Counseling*, Vol. 6, 1984, pp.155-9

——Teaching the Patient with Ischemic Heart Disease: A Systematic Approach to Instructional Design. *Patient Counseling and Health Education*, 3, 1981, pp. 57-62.

Griffith, Alison, "Mothering, Schooling, and Children's Development", in M. Campbell and Ann Manicom (eds.), *Knowledge, Experience and Ruling Relations: Studies in the Social Organization of Knowledge* (Toronto: University of Toronto Press, 1995), pp. 108-21.

Hall, Bud, "From Margins to Center? The Development and Purpose of Participatory Research," *The American Sociologist*, Vol. 23, No. 4, 1992, pp.15-28.

References

Hammersley, Martyn, and Paul Atkinson, *Ethnography: Principles in Practice*. London: Routledge, 1995, second edition.

Jakubec, Sonya, *Ordering Madness for the Social Organization of the World Mental Health: An Institutional Ethnography*, unpublished Master of Nursing thesis, Faculty of Human and Social Development, University of Victoria, 2001.

Jung, Karen, *The Social Organization of Power in the Academy's Disability Policy: Chronic Illness, Academic Accommodation and "Equity"*, unpublished Master of Arts thesis, Department of Sociology, University of Victoria, 2000.

Kivel, Paul, *Uprooting Racism: How White People Can Work for Racial Justice*, Gabriola Island, BC: New Society Press, 1996.

Kinsman, Gary, "Managing AIDS Organizing: 'Consultation,' 'Partnership,' and 'Responsibility' as Strategies of Regulation," in W.K. Carroll (ed.), *Organizing Dissent: Contemporary Social Movements in Theory and Practice* (Toronto: Garamond Press, 1997), second edition.

Latour, Bruno and Steve Woolgar, *Laboratory Life: The Construction of Scientific Facts*, Princeton: Princeton University Press, 1979.

Lomas, Jonathan, "Improving Research Dissemination and Uptake in the Health Sector: Beyond the Sound of One Hand Clapping," unpublished report prepared for the Advisory Committee on Health Services to the Federal/Provincial/Territorial Conference of Deputy Ministers, McMaster University, August 1997.

Manicom, Ann, "What's Health Got To Do With It? Class, Gender and Teacher's Work" in M. Campbell and Ann Manicom (eds.), *Knowledge, Experience and Ruling Relations: Studies in the Social Organization of Knowledge*, Toronto: University of Toronto Press, 1995, pp. 135-48.

McCoy, Liza, *Accounting Discourse and Textual Practices of Ruling: A Study of Institutional Transformation and Restructuring in Higher Education*, unpublished PhD dissertation, University of Toronto, 1999.

Miller, Rena, *Manageable Problems/Unmanageable Death: The Social Organization of Palliative Care*, unpublished MSW thesis, University of Victoria, 1997.

Moss, Pamela, *Placing Autobiography in Geography*, Syracuse: Syracuse University Press, 2001.

Mykhalovoskiy, Eric, "On the Uses of Health Services Research: Troubled Hearts, Care Pathways and Hospital Restructuring," *Studies in Cultures, Organizations and Societies*, (forthcoming).

——*Knowing Health Care/Governing Health Care: Exploring Health Research as Social Practice*, unpublished PhD dissertation, York University, 2000.

Ng, Roxana, *The Politics of Community Services: Immigrant Women, Class and State*, first edition, Toronto: Garamond Books,1988; second edition, Halifax: Fernwood Publishing, 1996.

Park, P., "The Discovery of Participatory Research as a New Scientific Paradigm: Personal and Intellectual Accounts", *The American Sociologist*, Vol. 23, No. 4, 1992, 29-31.

Pence, Ellen, Safety for Women in a Textually Mediated Legal System, Studies in Cultures, Organizations and Societies, Vol. X, No. x, 2001, pp. xx-xx.

——and Lizdas, K. *The Duluth Safety and Accountability Audit*, Duluth: Author, 1998

Prus, Robert, "Approaching the Study of Human Group Life: Symbolic Interaction and Ethnography", in M. Dietz, R. Prus and W. Shaffir (eds.), *Doing Everyday Life: Ethnography as Human Lived Experience* (Missisauga: Copp Clark Longman, 1994), pp. 10-29.

Purkis, Mary Ellen, "Embodied Knowledge: Organizational Technologies and Competence in Nursing Practice", in K. Teghtsoonian and M. Campbell, (eds.), *Theories for the Human Services* (forthcoming).

Rankin, Janet, *How Nurses Practice Health Care Reform: An Institutional Ethnography*, unpublished PhD Dissertation, University of Victoria, forthcoming.

——"Patient Satisfaction: Knowledge for Ruling Quality of Care", paper presented at Crossroads in Cultural Theory, Eighth International Conference, University of Birmingham, UK, June 2000.

Reinhartz, Shulamit, *Feminist Methods in Social Research*, New York: Oxford University Press, 1992.

Roberts, Helen (ed.), *Doing Feminist Research*, London: Routledge and Kegan Paul, 1981

Schreiber, Rita, "The 'How-to' of Grounded Theory: Avoiding the Pitfalls," in R.S. Schreiber and P.N. Stern (eds.), *Using Grounded Theory in Nursing* (New York: Springer, 2001), pp. 55-84.

Scott, Joan, "The Evidence of Experience," *Critical Inquiry*, Vol. 17, No. 3, 1991, pp. 773-97

Smith, Dorothy E., *Writing the Social: Critique, Theory and Investigations*, Toronto: University of Toronto Press, 1999.

——*The Conceptual Practices of Power: A Feminist Sociology of Knowledge*, Toronto: University of Toronto Press, 1990a

——*Texts, Facts and Femininity: Exploring the Relations of Ruling*, London: Routledge, 1990b

——*The Everyday World as Problematic: A Feminist Sociology*, Toronto: University of Toronto Press and Northeastern Press, 1987.

——"The Renaissance of Women" in Ursula Franklin, et al. (eds.), *Knowledge Reconsidered: A Feminist Overview*, Ottawa: Canadian Research Institute for the Advancement of Women, 1984, pp.3-14.

——"Text-mediated Social Organization," *International Social Science Journal*, Vol. 36, 1984, pp. 59-75.

——*Feminism and Marxism: A Place to Begin, A Way to Go*, Vancouver: New Star Books, 1977.

——The Social Construction of Documentary Reality, *Sociological Inquiry*, Vol. 44, No. 4, 1975, pp. 257-67.

Smith George W. "Accessing Treatments: Managing the AIDS Epidemic in Ontario," in M. Campbell and A. Manicom (eds.), *Knowledge, Experience and Ruling Relations: Studies in the Social Organization of Knowledge* (Toronto: University of Toronto Press, 1995), pp. 18-34.

——"Political Activist as Ethnographer" *Social Problems* Vol. 37, 1990, pp.629-48.

——"AIDS Treatment Deficits: An Ethnographic Study of the Management of the AIDS Epidemic, the Ontario Case", a paper presented at the fifth International AIDS conference, Montreal, Canada, 1989.

Stanley, Liz and Sue Wise, *Breaking Out Again: Feminist Ontology and Epistemology*, London: Routledge, 1993.

Swift, Karen, *Manufacturing Bad Mothers: A Critical Perspective on Child Neglect*, Toronto: University of Toronto Press, 1995

Thomas, Jim, *Doing Critical Ethnography*, Newbury Park, CA: Sage, 1993.

Whittaker, Elvi, "The Contribution of Herbert Blumer to Anthropology," in Mary L. Dietz, Robert Prus and William Shaffir, (eds.), *Doing Everyday Life: Ethnography as Human Lived Experience* (Mississauga, Ont.: Copp Clark Longman, 1994).

Notes

Introduction

1. The books by Smith referred to are *The Everyday World as Problematic: A Feminist Sociology*, published simultaneously by the University of Toronto Press and Northeastern University Press,1987; *The Conceptual Practices of Power: A Feminist Sociology of Knowledge*, University of Toronto Press, 1990; *Texts, Facts and Femininity: Exploring the Relations of Ruling*, Routledge, 1990; and *Writing the Social: Critique, Theory and Investigations*, University of Toronto Press, 1999.

Chapter One

2. See Chapter Four for how a literature review contributes to an institutional ethnography.
3. Richard Darville is a professor in the School of Linguistics and Applied Language Studies, Carleton University, Ottawa. He worked as a literacy teacher and advocate in Vancouver, while and for a number of years after completing a doctorate in Sociology at UBC. He continues to be a literacy theorist.
4. By the time she was a graduate student, Jan had moved into different employment.
5. The assignment is a readings journal that asks students to summarize assigned readings to capture the writer's message, and to use textual clues to identify and document the writer's social location, and the intended audience. Then they chronicle their own response to the reading's message, identifying whatever personal experiences seem to relate to their reading. They are encouraged to explore for themselves any connection they discover between the meaning they make from the reading and their own backgrounds. The assignment offers the opportunity for students to recognize knowing as socially organized, located, and embodied.

Chapter Three

6. Technical skills of reading and summarizing are also taught, to encourage students to be attentive to issues of accuracy, for instance. For ideas about improving technical reading skills, I rely on Giltrow's *Academic Writing: Writing and Reading across the Disciplines* (1995).
7. In addition to the Smith books, see M. DeVault's *Liberating Method* (1999) and DeVault and McCoy's chapter in J. Gubrium and J. Holstein (1995). Campbell and Manicom's edited collec-

tion (1995) offers an extensive reference list. Since that book was published several important doctoral theses have been completed, notably McCoy 1999, Mykhalovskiy 2000.

8. Dorothy Smith discusses this in *The Conceptual Practices of Power*, pp. 95-6, where she says, "Rules of confidentiality, corporate ownership of information, corporate systems of data storage, and so forth, provide specifically for the exclusive control of texts, keeping them within the scope of specific interpretive contexts of reading and use."

Chapter Five

9. Marj DeVault uses this word to talk about her analytic process in *Liberating Methodology.* She says: "It refers to a kind of investigation that begins with what can be seen and heard but holds in mind the sense that there is more to find – like the archeologist's knowledge that any bone or fragment of pottery, for instance, points towards a complete organism or object (p. 56).

10. Bell's field of study was textual, whereas for many institutional ethnographies, the setting is a workplace, a home, or myriad places where human action can be observed. Texts offer the same opportunities to study social relations as do other kinds of socially-organized phenomena. The theory behind any kind of institutional ethnography is the same and so is the methodology. Institutional ethnographers would look at any site of study to understand the social relations that organize "what actually happens" in it.

Chapter Six

11. The final text has a shorter version of this account of her data sources.

12. Funds for the three-year project were granted by the BC Health Research Foundation, the Social Sciences and Humanities Research Council of Canada and Human Resources Development, Canada, and the Vancouver Foundation.

13. Betty Tate, MN and Brenda Copeland, MA, staffed the project as research coordinators. Their skill and experience in community development kept the project in balance, and their dedication to the negotiated tenets of the research made an enormous contribution to its success.

14. The first research team members included D. Darlington, M. Essery, J. Hughes, S. Kimpson, L. Melchior, C. Robinson, and J. Toone. After six months, health care workers C. Preston, D. Bailey, L. Carlson, K. Lazaro, C. Middleton were selected and later, Dr. M.E. Purkis joined the team.

15. See Campbell, Copeland and Tate, "Taking the standpoint of people with disabilities in research: Experiences with participation", 1998.

16. A working group of research team members conceptualized the game and Luke Melchior designed its material form as a board game. The game has been used in a workshop "Thinking Differently and Acting Differently" offered successfully to many community and academic groups by the research team. Work is proceeding on commercializing it.

17. Kinsman notes "One major federal initiative, the Krever Commission (1994-5), which had still not reported by early 1997, became the first federal commission of inquiry into AIDS-related matters, focusing on how it was that more than a thousand haemophiliacs and others were infected through the blood supply" in the 1980s (Kinsman, 219).

Index

AGMV Marquis

MEMBER OF SCABRINI MEDIA

Quebec, Canada
2004